ROMANCING
THE HILARITY

MY JOURNEY TO ROMANTIC IDENTITY,
INCLUDING MOST
OF MY WRONG TURNS

Morris A. DuBose v.3.0

Most of what you'll read is completely true—some of it cobbled together from bits and pieces of memory. A few of the characters are compilations of two or three real people. Many of the names in the work have been changed.

The majority of this collection was written as individual essays and blog posts. While edited for quality, some of the language reflects my state of mind at the time of original writing.

ISBN: 978-0-9904611-0-4

Thanks!

I'd like to thank all the women who've helped me learn about…women. Specifically, I have to thank Sarah, Allison, Abbie, Liz, Betsy, Kathi, Jennifer, Sarah, Megan, Abby, Megan, Sue, Lindsay, and Mrs. Hill (my first crush).

Jeremy, Dan, Brian, Brian, Phil, Josh

Pandora (for the ultimate work tunes)
Barbara and Allan Pease (for all of their works)

And, as clichéd as it sounds, I want to thank God.

An Open Letter to My Wife

My Dear Wife Jess,

Without you, this book would be a handful of blog posts, and incomprehensible thoughts which my unfocused mind would never have synthesized into usable language. you have been amazing in this book writing process. You encouraged me to write. And, also to take healthy breaks and get out of the house when I started to collapse in on myself.

It's been a year, and we're still discovering how steep the learning curve is. I fell for your creativity, enthusiasm, sense of adventure, faith, and conviction. Thanks for bringing those things to bear in our relationship.

Without you, I'm a boat in a storm. All my efforts are aimless and futile.

Love,

Morris

Contents

Preface

I am the kind of guy who doesn't mind holding a purse for his mom, sister or friend while out shopping. I am also quite capable of picking up tampons from the store—and doing so without grumbling or complaining. I understand the musical appeal of Kelly Clarkson, Pink, and Michael Bublé. I like to cuddle. I'm not much of a sports fanatic. I always put the seat down. I actually like the colors pink and purple and the essence of fresh flowers. And I'm not too bad in the kitchen either.

For these reasons, along with other more substantial ones, I figured it wouldn't be that much of a stretch to think I'd do okay as a significant other. Though I have learned, that for all my points of aptitude, there are still a lot of things in which I have no clue about.

After years of dating, crushing, rejecting, pining, social media stalking, "winking," *Quick Matching, Plenty of Fishing,* avoiding, repressing, declaring, denying, and more—I got married in June of 2013. And, by and large, it's been awesome.

Some days it feels like I have this romance thing figured out. Other days, I feel like I shouldn't have been allowed to marry; the thing about marriage is that you get the opportunity to be introduced to a whole different level of intelligence. I feel like I studied for my Lit final all year; and at test time, they asked the essay question from the study guide, and then threw in one of the millennium prize problems on the end.

Everything about romance is about a half step away from insanity if it isn't already insane. Therefore, this isn't a guide—as it's dangerous to write a guide to madness—even madness that is truly joy. But I do have a few stories to tell and I hope you can learn something from them, or at least laugh. Actually, I just want you to laugh.

It's Complicated

Every relationship status on Facebook should end with "it's complicated." Let's be honest, whatever point of the spectrum in which you happen to find yourself, it's either *complicated*, or you're lying to yourself. It doesn't mean it's bad; there's just another layer. And I have news for you; status is like Shrek... I mean an ogre... I mean an onion, besides the fact that they may stink and make you cry, when you peel away the last layer, there may not be anything left.[1]

Single

The "Single" status—somebody's dream is someone else's nightmare. Dane Cook talks about singleness in terms of not being invited to the party that everyone else seems to be attending. You really want to be in that party. But, do you?...*It's complicated.*[2] Some days, you're living the life, enjoying the time and space you have all to yourself. You're thrilled 'cause you only shell out for one ticket leaving you enough money to have all the popcorn you want for yourself. If you date, it's casual. Everything you do seems fun. The sky is the limit.

Other times, every moment of singleness feels like you're stranded in the valley of the shadow of death wishing a good neighbor like State Farm will come along and rescue you from the darkness. Your own bed feels a bit too cold. You want to ride along with someone else, even if they drive from the passenger's side. You wish there was another hand in your popcorn bucket, even if someone spills a few kernels in your lap...or maybe you don't. When chatting with a stranger of the opposite sex, you spend at least half the time figuring out if they are flirting with you, or really just asking if you'd like to add an apple pie for a dollar. Every interaction is a chance to flirt...I mean, fall in love... I mean, get rejected...*It's complicated.*

Then, of course, there's the standard incarnation that it's just complicated. And that covers a multitude of sins. Unrequited love? Friends with benefits? *It's complicated.*

You dumped your partner; it was supposed to be temporary to make them miss you, so you could get your way, and now s/he won't take you back? Everyone wants you except the one you want? You think you're dating, but are not sure if the other person feels the same way, so you change your status hoping she'll maybe take the hint? *It's complicated.*

You just got out of a serious relationship—and you are really interested in a new person—but you don't want to date just yet? *It's complicated.* The two of you have been spending time together, one minute she's really into her career (or school) right now, but then the next she is all sentimental about your relationship needing to be a priority. So just when you think you're maybe making headway and the relationship is actually amounting to something, you find out you're her action on the side. You're riding pine on the sideline. Her star player just found out about you, too. Despite all that, you're still on her hook. You still like dressing with her team, a lot more than you should...Don't judge me!...*It's complicated!*

Then, of course there are THE statuses: *In a relationship* or *engaged* or *married*, which take complicated to a whole new level.

Dating

Usually, you feel like you've known each other forever. You've got this pseudo-psychic teamwork thing going on, until you don't. Then you're staring at the other person, wondering, *who on earth am I talking to?*—and end up at each other's throats for misinterpreting one another's thoughts.

Not only are you concerned about getting to know your new love interest, you're trying to figure out the drill with each of your families—wanting to make a good impression, but not wanting to kiss ass. You put on slacks and a tie, but stop short of siding with the folks on politics and religion. The whole thing is an awkward mess of telling the person you're dating what you think they want to hear, yet showing them more and more of who you really are.

Hitch says it well, "She may not want the whole truth, but she does want the real you. She may not want to see it all at once, but she does want to see it." Then of course, there's the pièce de résistance, 'cause, at the end of the day, "it is your job not to mess it up!"[3] So, you're trying to be Superman, Clark Kent, and Lex Luthor all at the same time. *It's complicated...*And even that's putting it mildly.

Engaged

Then, somebody pops the question. "How about we do this dance until one of us kicks the bucket?" So now you're trying to sort out what comes next. You're picking out flowers. Your families are meeting up, and you're not sure how all of this is going to play out. You

don't think your uncle will mesh with...well, anyone in
your fiancé's family... or anyone in a civilized society.
Your bride hates your best man. You're pretty sure
you saw your groom checking out the in-from-out-of-
town bridesmaid. Whose things are going to stay and
what's getting tossed for good? And, there's the stifling
truth that a whole lot of things which have never been
in the same room, will be living under the same roof.
If that's not complicated, I don't know what is.

Married

I now pronounce you happily confused. You're
married. Suddenly you're sharing life in a way you
never have. You have someone to shop with, to eat
with, to think with, to drive with, to sleep with, and to
fight with. You learn about each other in a fresh and
exciting way. She likes the blinds closed at night; you
like them open. He listens to audio books and you
don't want him to play them on the house stereo
'cause they make you sleepy. You learn about yourself
in a completely new way. You really like to cuddle, but
only for a little while. But, she doesn't like it when you
extricate yourself. Sex is new, exciting, and
emotionally loaded. Sometimes it's awesome, other
times, a joke pops into your head and you laugh at the
absolute worst time. You try to explain that you
weren't entirely in the moment, but now, it's really
complicated.

Ten years and a whole lot of early mornings and late
dinners later, it's blurry all over again. When the
things that were cute become the things which grind
your gears? *It's complicated.* The movie *Mr. & Mrs.
Smith* has one great example after another regarding
the normalization of the craziness that is two lives

smashed together.[4] A linchpin of this particular dinner scene discussion is the addition of peas. And, the entire conversation serves as a relational shield between the two of them and their mass of hidden secrets. Do they love each other? Yeah. Underneath the rubble of faded passion, divergent dreams, cultural variances, nervous tics, unnatural habits— they love each other. But, you have to get past the dirty clothes on the floor, the unprompted sob fests, his bad taste in clothing, her extreme attention to detail, and everything else, to find the fact that she likes lilacs over roses ten to one, or that he always smiles when you cheer for his team, and that some things you do never cease to ease your partner off of the edge when they've had a rough day. It all sucks, until that special someone holds you. *It's complicated.*

So, basically, if you're alone, together, in love, in hate, seeing each other socially, bumping into each other in the street, dating, fighting, flirting, cleanly broken, or not quite over each other, married, pining, engaged, or just plain dating? *It's complicated.*

The Birds
&
The Bees

To paraphrase The Late Mitch Hedberg (may he rest
in peace), I used to be a nerd. I still am, but I used to
be, too. When I was about ten, I started to get curious.
While Kevin McCallister and my peers were
rummaging through the locked chests and sock
drawers of their older brothers and fathers, I wasn't.[5]
I waited until no one was around, walked into our
living room, pulled out the "S" volume of our family's
1992 edition of the *World Book Encyclopedia* and
flipped it open to "Sex." I read the following, "See:
Sexual Intercourse." BAM!! I learned something
already. So after turning to "Sexual Intercourse," I
read the article, and learned that it had something to
do with "privates" and... really, I didn't get anything
useful out of it. Thanks a lot World Book Encyclopedia
Company.

In the fifth grade, my parents sent me to a little
Christian school. If you went to a Christian school, it
was just like you remember. If you didn't it was
basically the movie *Saved!* without the pregnant girl,
the Jewish girl, or the kid in the wheelchair; which is
a shame, 'cause they were awesome and would have
made my school experience way more exciting.[6]
Marilyn Manson did go to my school, but that was
before my time. And, there once was a sex scandal, but
that was after my time. So while I was there, the only
thing notable about the school was that it was a
Christian school— still rather noteworthy when you

have to tackle something like Sex Ed. It's also a big deal when you have a science class where you can't ask questions about evolution. But, in middle school, Sex Ed seemed way more important.

In the sixth grade, my classmates and I had the opportunity to study the book, *Preparing for Adolescence,* by Dr. James Dobson. Now, if you're not familiar with him, Dr. Dobson is the founder of Focus on the Family, who left that ultra-conservative organization to found another more conservative organization with even less oversight and academic accountability. Along the way, this guy wrote a book about our bodies, the changes within, and the emotions associated with them.[7] It could pretty much be summed up as: Chew ice chips and pray until you get married; because if you touch yourself or have sex before you get married, you'll become the next Ted Bundy, and the state of Florida will put you down like a dog and your soul will burn. And, I'm paraphrasing.

Early on in our study of this book, our teacher, Mr. T, opened up the floor for preliminary questions. "Ask about whatever," he said. His proposal met with deafening silence. It's not that we weren't interested; it's just that this particular teacher had a little bit of a temper. He didn't respond well to things he didn't like. One day when the class was a little restless, Mr. T famously slammed a textbook on a table and shouted, "Shut the door!" to one of the other students. The book slam was more striking than it may have been otherwise because of his reddening face and the bulging veins. You could see him choking back far harsher language and a much louder yell. It really came out, "SHUT THE...DOOR!!"And for the

WASPy** kids in that class, that was quite overwhelming. But, this same "Shut-the-door" man wanted us to ask him any question we wanted, about puberty? We passed on that offer. But as a teacher, he couldn't let it go. He called out a specific student by name. "[Student] I can tell you have a question, just ask it."

"No Thanks."

"Just ask!"

"I really don't feel..."

"[Student] ask your question!"

My classmate looks down at his desk and mutters.

"What was that?" Mr. T demands.

"When I get married, will I stop having wet dreams?"

The room actually managed to go even quieter as Mr. T sent one of the five iciest glares I've witnessed across the room to the student.

"Get out... just, go to the office, right now..."

And, that in a nutshell was my Sex Ed experience in a Christian private school.

Well...If the private school system fails you, you can always turn to your family, right? The "birds and the bees" talk wasn't one of the things which I looked

---

*White Anglo-Saxon Protestant

forward to having. It's not that my dad isn't a good dude. In fact, he's one of the better people I know. He's thoughtful, helpful, and does well with most of the basic dad stuff. He taught me how to throw a football, change my oil, and tie a tie. But romance? Not his strong suit—nor were the emotions that went along with it. So, telling me about women and sex and all that jazz was going to be as tough as a horsefly filling in on a bee's day off.

While reading a book in my room one summer afternoon just prior to high school, I was surprised when my dad walked in. It wasn't necessarily surprising that he was in my room, but he was fairly good about knocking. The fact that he didn't, now worried me more than a little. He loomed uncomfortably in my doorway for a few moments, while I bookmarked my spot with my finger. "Well...," he began, "you're old enough that you have probably figured your own attitudes on dating and stuff like that."

"I guess," I responded shrugging into my book and avoiding eye contact while bracing for what would likely be the most awkward conversation of my life to that point.

"Well, okay then," he said. Then as suddenly as he'd come, he was gone.
And that, in a nutshell, was the rest of my experience with Sex Ed.

I'm not entirely sure how I made it to adulthood.

The Road to Color; or
Kissing Dating Goodbye

Have you ever had that moment, when you look at the mirror and almost catch yourself off guard? For a split second your brain doesn't assign all your existing thoughts and opinions about you to your reflection. You see yourself completely differently than you ever have before; or at least, differently than you usually do. It's odd how much of who we are comes from who we think we are. I'm not going to get all, "The Secret" on you, I promise. I'll tell you a story and maybe you can develop your own little kitschy philosophy.

Closing in on thirty, I think I'm Pandora's Box, minus the evil. When I was young, I was sure I was a bundled assortment of concepts, ideals, morals, stereotypes, etc. But surety is a silly kind of thought. I thought I was simple. I dressed in black pants and gray turtlenecks quite often. Seriously, for a lengthy stretch, I owned two pairs of black slacks, three pairs of black jeans, and four different gray turtlenecks. I could mix it up, though; I had a handful of black-and-white turtlenecks. I did have a hunter green one that I whipped out when I was feeling crazy. By middle school, I started wearing random Christian graphic tees over my turtlenecks, not every day, but from time to time. Most of which had white, black, or gray as their base colors. My Pandora's fashion box was packed tightly, once it opened, there was no going back.

I liked my world like I preferred my clothing—structured, functional, simple, and largely black and white. The only thing that didn't match, between my philosophy and attire, was my appreciation for shades of gray. Not long ago, I stumbled across a personal statement, which I wrote during my early high school years, which illustrated the fact that I definitely preferred all my moral and personal issues clearly cut. Life was so much easier when I could just stay on my side of the line.

Like many good evangelical youths in the late nineties, I kissed dating goodbye. Joshua Harris wrote a book that took the Christian youth sub-subculture by storm. He advocated an alternative to the conventional system of modern dating, in the interesting ostensibly archaic model of courtship. It caused waves in the entire Christian world. Some people hated it. Some used it more like guidelines than actual rules; which, according to the author, was the intention. Many others used it as a way to develop restrictive and sometimes truly overbearing rules for date-like activities in groups, etc. I wouldn't say I created legalistic rules, but I was definitely one of those people who loved it.

To be perfectly honest, I was predisposed to kiss dating goodbye. I was an opinionated, conservative, well-read, reasonably well-spoken, evangelical, ex-homeschooled kid in junior high school; which meant I knew everything. I'd actually been advocating for a friend-oriented alternative to dating since I was in the fifth grade. I wrote an eloquent, if condescending, essay to that effect for an electronic forum hosted by a friend. And, all throughout high school, I maintained that I wanted to have at least one year of friendship with any girl I was interested in "courting" before I actually moved into the overt, romantic entanglement of a relationship.

During college, as many others have experienced, some of my ideals began to turn a little gray. But, my theoretical and practical abstinence from the traditional dating world actually lasted into my post-secondary life. It worked out well, since even as a child, I got along much better with women than I did with men. So, in keeping with the spirit of my "no dating" stance, I cultivated a circle of friends which always included a few young women with whom I could see myself building a relationship, and possibly… hopefully, a life. In my collegiate junior year, however, that theory fell apart.

I'd been harboring some tender feelings for a friend of mine for quite a while and I finally decided to express them to her. The revelation of my genuine sentiments resulted not only in her surprise, but also a lack of reciprocation, which exposed a massive gap in my theory: Both parties have to have, in advance, subscribed to the philosophy of looking for a partner within their existing friend group. If either one does not hold that same ideal, then not making your romantic intentions known, stunts the potential for an affectionate development. This paradigm shift is problematic for a young man who has had an answer to every hypothetical question that the skeptics posed to him. And, very suddenly, one more thing became clearly gray.

As my philosophy grayed; my wardrobe erupted more color. I spent the remaining few weeks of that semester reflecting on how un-simple everything in life was turning out to be; even and especially romance. At the same time, my gray, black, and white look started feeling disingenuous. Despite being dealt an emotional blow to a fairly integral aspect of my worldview, a tiny part of me felt free and dynamic. The first thing I did when I returned from school that year? Walk into an Express and buy a brown, tattersall-patterned shirt, it fit me like a glove, and even served to bring out my eyes. I strolled out of that store, into a world of color and never looked back. From there, I dove into pink, and even went so far as to explore multi-colored stripes. By the end of that summer I had blues, purples, and greens. Today, bright colors, pastels, patterns, and accessories are my signature.

Since making the dramatic switch from monochrome to Technicolor attire, my ideas are now nearly all within the gray area. I'm convinced that people will take wildly diverse roads to relational satisfaction. I am disinclined to assert one path's rightness and wrongness. If you're doing your best to stay out of abusive relationships, then I think that's a good start. The rest will likely be trial and error. There are a great deal of insights which people must grasp on their own, especially me. Experience was a merciless teacher, but I learned my lessons well.

So, after college I dated. I dated casually, and I dated seriously. All the while, I had a lot of fun doing it. But, I know that refraining from dating up through college was a vital part of my journey. If you think that's your path, I'm happy for you. But, I think I would have turned out okay if I hadn't been obstinately single. I have far fewer rules to share than I did back then. But tomorrow, who knows what I'll think.

The Heart You Break
May Be Your Own

Starting college away from everything I knew was
amazing—new activities, new adventures, new
classes, and best of all, new people. My first crush in
college was fresh and exciting. The first time I saw her
she was on stage singing at the "Welcome Week"
talent show. She was dynamic and engaging with just
enough self-deprecation to make her likable. And, like
her...I did.

We met the next day at a campus café and she was
even more vibrant up close, she had dramatic
ambition and the personality to match. I come from a
fairly large family, so her larger-than-life nature made
me feel instantly at ease.

We had an easy acquaintanceship which quickly
turned into a friendship and by the end of the week we
were the de facto leaders of a small band of new
friends. In the ensuing months we spent a substantial
amount of time together, both in the company of

others and alone. There were never any romantic overtures, but I always had a little bit of a crush on her. Sometimes I would weigh the pros and cons of wandering past the borders of a crush. And though it never seemed far from the realm of possibility, I never did.

During those special weekends hosted to keep students distracted, and families involved, her parents came to the campus and she of course showed them off to our little group. They were offbeat and delightful, with personalities just as big as their daughter's. We took them to dinner at the dining hall; they took us out to a restaurant. We played games and even saw a play. We couldn't have fit much more fun in that weekend even if we would have used a shoehorn.

With her parents homeward bound, our group dispersed and the two of us headed back toward our dorms. As we approached her door, she started, "Oh, my gosh! I have to tell you the funniest thing." I followed her into her room as she continued, barely able to contain her smile, "After dinner, my mom said that you and I should date." And, at this point, her efforts failed—she dissolved into laughter.

My only salvation comes from the fact that as she delivered her punch line, she was facing away from me, tossing a few papers on her desk. Horrified, I replaced my visage with one of amused shock and a desperate chuckle emerged just as she turned to face me. Not fully trusting my voice, I exhaled, "What?"

Her response, "I know, right?" is the last thing I heard before the ringing in my ears made it impossible to do anything other than watch her mouth move and nod in agreement. I "remembered" something I had to do before it became too late, and excused myself for the night. I walked out with measured steps and pulled the door closed behind me, still smiling.

In the emptiness of the hallway, the gut-punched breath I was hiding was finally expelled, and tears came to my eyes. My smile, however, did not falter until the safety of my own room, when my well of tears finally overflowed, spilling silently down my cheek.

I'd just failed a test by experience, the teacher, with more lessons to follow.

Cardinal

I want to be in a relationship. Most days, I'd like for it to be romantic. But some days it needn't be.

Sitting in a café, absorbed in a book, I glance up and out of the window. I notice a bright red cardinal—standing in stark contrast to the heavily-clouded evening's pseudo-light—staring in the window at me. "Come see! Come see!" I wanted to shout to someone...Anyone. But, the older man and the younger woman were totally immersed in their coffee. The young man behind me is on wireless life support, embedding every fiber of his being into his computer, and the barista is too far away.
The cardinal, tired of his perch and staring at me, flutters off to his next engagement. Maybe home to tell his family about the lonely human from the coffee shop.

-Journal Entry May 2008

Becoming Prince Charming

With a few notable exceptions, my closest friends are women. I just happen to get along with them better. The complexity. The self-reflection. The fashion sense. There's just more room in the ranks of women for all of my idiosyncrasies. So ever since forever, I've been welcomed in as one of the girls. As a direct result, despite the immense complexities among individual women, I've had the opportunity to observe coalescing patterns. These patterns, coupled with friends, provide me with frequent and invaluable feedback.

So between this life experience and the small mountain of books I've read, I perform relational maintenance or at least damage control quite well. And sometimes, damage control is all we can hope for. I possess the qualities of a good friend and—I believe—an okay partner. The women in my life have joked, asked, and at times flatly insisted that I teach a course on women in which I help guys of all ages evolve into the men that women want to date…or at least, take a step toward an ideal.

As much as I enjoy teaching—and being right—I just don't think I could actually teach that class. Every day I learn something new, most of which I had no previous idea—it's like the idea in philosophy where a man is in the dark. The man in the dark has a hand light, and as he learns the circle of light becomes bigger. But, the growing circle of light only serves to expose how immensely vast the enveloping darkness is.

Many people have the wrong impression about flirting. The words 'flirting' and 'seduction' get used interchangeably, but they are not true synonyms.

Flirt (v) – to court triflingly or act amorously without serious intentions

Seduce (v) – to persuade or induce to have sexual intercourse.[8]

The confusion is understandable because there is significant overlap. The same way people can start out clowning around and then end up beating the hell out of one another, flirting and seduction are different exits on the same freeway… And, I really enjoy driving.

No one in my family is promiscuous, but we tend to be enthusiastic people who like having fun. My younger brother, Phil, was born flirting. He's just smooth. With an unbelievably easy smile, the confidence rolls off of him in waves. Phil is magic. He leans in and ardently seizes your hand when you meet him. When he jokes around, he makes you feel like you have known each other forever. And when you're talking to Phil, you're the only person in the world. That is flirting.

Making people feel unbelievably special is a superpower. In Nora Ephron's film, *You've Got Mail,* Joe Fox (Tom Hanks) convinces Rose (Sara Ramirez), the cashier in the "cash only" line to take a credit card from the deeply frustrated Kathleen Kelly (Meg Ryan). But not by ranting, arguing, threatening, rationally persuading, crying or begging; instead he makes eye contact, tells a joke, draws out Rose's holiday spirit, and reaffirms her humanity during the ironically inhuman time which is the holiday rush. "Rose, that is a great name. I'm Joe. This is Kathleen[...] Happy Thanksgiving. It's your turn to say 'Happy Thanksgiving' back." He got what he wanted; a zip of the card reader. And she got what she wanted; a momentary reprieve from the hectic yet monotonous shift at the checkout line.[9] His special ability to make her feel good could qualify him to be an X-Man.

My brother Phil was born with that power. We stopped for a fill-up one afternoon during high school. I walked in to pay for the gas. Phil walked in with twenty-five cents and a smile. I pumped and Phil chatted. When I finished with the car, Phil walked out of the station. He didn't have his quarter, but he did have coffee and a bear claw from the in-station Dunkin' Donuts. Needless to say, Phil was great at those "Bigger and Better" challenges.

Don't get the wrong idea about Phil, he isn't a crazy scammer or even a serial monogamist—he just flirts. When our pastor took us to see King Kong, neither of us was particularly interested in the film. Shortly after the dinosaur fight, Phil decided he'd rather invest the remainder of his 187 minutes elsewhere. After the film, we hooked back up at the card and flower shop where Phil had purchased a small plant to be gifted and was charming the cashier. Watching them, you could see easy, fun conversation and no pressure. He just made her feel good.

Even though I wasn't born with that skill, I put a lot of time into studying it. It didn't hurt that I had a few great case studies in my life. I also read and tried and erred a lot. Sometimes, I even flirted over the topic of studying flirting.

Once, I was attending a party at a mystery dinner theater. At the beginning of the show, the characters were making their way from table to table to engage the guests. Two of them were chatting with our group when one of them saw my copy of *Flirting 101*[10] by Michelle Lewis and Andrew Bryant, and laser-locked onto it. I could have been mortified. I could have hidden it. I could have gotten angry. Instead, I joked about how much we all need help with people sometimes. I pulled it out and read an excerpt or two, then handed the book over to them. They even used it in the evening's frivolities. And, all of the characters spent a disproportionate amount of time at our table, having fun.

No matter why I'm flirting at that moment, I try to make sure that I only keep going as long as we're both having fun. I make sure my posture is unthreatening, keeping a few healthy feet of space between the two of us; I even try to add a physical barrier, like a table or counter to the mix. I want to give her as few possible reasons to put or keep her guard up. Because, let's face it, despite the prevailing idea that "it's hard out here for a pimp," it's actually hard out here for women.[11] Most guys don't think about how scary it is to have a strange man ask her out, much less how scary it must be to accept. Stand-up comedian, Louis C.K., illustrates this concept, "If you're a guy, try to imagine that you could only date a half bear, half lion."[12] Think about that when you're looming over a girl asking, "Can I have yo' number?"

With that in mind, I'm always looking out for both verbal and non-verbal cues. Sometimes you need to cut bait and run. Like when you ask a half serious, half funny question to the girl standing next to you in the book store, and she responds with an unsmiling and extremely curt reply while subtly, reorienting her body away from you; Thank her, graciously, and return to your own browsing (maybe in a different aisle).

If, on the other hand, a woman you approach responds positively, just simply refrain from being overwhelming. Think of it like the old kids' game, "Mother, May I?" The kids who won at "Mother May I?" are the ones who asked to take "normal steps" and "baby steps." It was the people always asking to take "super-incredible giant steps" that had their requests rejected, or worse, sent back from whence they came.

I'm not saying that every time you use healthy moderation, you'll win. It's 2009. Dan, my lifelong friend and roommate, and I are going to see the movie *Watchmen* with Joe, a co-worker. As we settle in for the comic-to-screen saga, I notice a cute girl walk in and sit down about eight rows closer to the screen. Not my taste in seat selection but, I'm not stubborn. For the duration of the movie I have one eye on the story and the other on the girl.

Unfortunately for me, the credits are barely rolling when the girl makes a beeline for the door. Despite being a black man in my mid-twenties, I do a decent job of making myself unassuming. Alas, no matter how unassuming you are, chasing a girl out of a darkened theater definitely constitutes taking a "super-incredible giant step." In most cases, it also constitutes a felony. And in a rich, Maryland suburb of D.C., if I came running out of the theater after a little white girl, they'd probably just ask questions later. So, I walk with the guys. We do so casually but I shuffle them along, just in case. When we get to the top of the escalator, I peel off and power walk to the door... and there she is.

She's facing the parking lot. And startling her under these circumstances would also pose a risk, albeit a much smaller one with almost no possibility of jail time. So I walk about a yard to her left and into her field of vision. I gain eye contact and gesture with my head back toward the theater,

 "Watchmen?" I asked.

"Yup," she replied.

"What'd you think?" I turned to face her.

"I liked it. It was a little long, but it was good."

It was better than a one word answer, but she didn't turn from the parking lot. She could have been looking for a ride or reticent to engage me. I don't want to press my luck, so I continue facing her, but don't move closer.

I'm not actually sure how I am progressing on the path toward inducing a smile. And, as I'm preparing to ask another open-ended question, Joe bursts through the doors of the theater and threads himself between me and the mystery girl. Turning his back fully on the girl, Joe asks me if I have a light. I hand him my Zippo as she steps off the curb. And by the time I extricate myself from his enthusiastic movie review, she's lost in a sea of cars. Sometimes your friends are your wingmen-- other times they are the misguided missiles bringing down your jet.

My failure notwithstanding, the guidelines remain the same:

Don't invade her personal space.
Do smile, and keep your body open.
Do make it a game.
Don't take a mile when she gives you an inch.
Do be considerate.
Do be complimentary but totally sincere.

The day Kate and I met, my Starbucks was packed— every one of my people-watching spots as well as all the comfy chairs are occupied. There's one zoo chair in the middle of the store. You know the chair. It's at the intersection of the people walking in the door, the back of the ever growing line, and the place where people wait impatiently for their orders to come up. As a result, when sitting there, you feel like you are a menagerie animal that the idle patrons analyze and mentally critique for their own entertaining pleasure.

Obviously, not wanting that spot, I grab my drink and head outside.

Though, most of the outdoor spots are also taken, there's an open seat at a table just off the sidewalk. The cute blonde occupying the other chair—and scribbling away in her notebook—seems as if she wouldn't mind sharing the table. I stroll over, not quickly, but with purpose. When I stop, the table, the empty seat, and my book are all between me and the woman.

"I'm looking for a place to read. Any chance I can borrow this chair?" When she looks up I can tell that she's a little more intense than I first thought. Nevertheless, she smiled up at me.

"If you want," she replied casually.

"Thanks. It's more crowded than usual today." I say, sitting down. I open up my book as she returns to her writing. For about fifteen minutes, I read and she writes, but I glance up regularly and somewhat furtively to look at her. I say somewhat, because I want to get caught, but I don't want to upset her flow. I only want to talk, if she does. After 15 minutes, she looks right at my book, "'*How to Buy a Love of Reading*,' that's kind of a weird title. Is it interesting?"

"It's a lot different than I expected it to be. It's a bit darker than it sounded." Pointing to her notebook, I refocus on her, "Taking notes on the world?"

"Yeah, I have a lot of stuff on my mind, and I wanted to get it down on paper."

"Makes sense to me. I write all the time. Your notebook is half the reason I sat next to you." The two of us joked and chatted for about an hour. I bought her a refill of her drink and asked for her number. And even though I crossed from totally playful to something more substantial, I kept it super light, and just offered to have coffee with her, in the same place, the next day.

Meeting new people and making them feel great is one of the best things I've experienced. In his 1936, bestselling book, *How to Win Friends and Influence People,* Dale Carnegie has some great things to say about making people feel good about themselves.

> *I was waiting in line to register a letter in the post office at Thirty-third Street and Eighth Avenue in New York. I noticed that the clerk appeared to be bored with the job—weighing envelopes, handing out stamps, making change, issuing receipts—the same monotonous grind year after year. So I said to myself: "I am going to try to make that clerk like me. Obviously, to make him like me, I must say something nice, not about myself, but about him[...]*
> *I told this story once in public and a man asked me afterwards:*
> *"'What did you want to get out of him?"*
>
> *What was I trying to get out of him!!! What was I trying to get out of him!!! If we are so contemptibly selfish that we can't radiate a little happiness and pass on a bit of honest appreciation without trying to get something out of the other person in return—if our souls are no bigger than sour crab apples, we shall*

meet with the failure we so richly deserve. Oh yes, I did want something out of that chap. I wanted something priceless. And I got it. I got the feeling that I had done something for him without his being able to do anything whatever in return for me. That is a feeling that flows and sings in your memory long after the incident is past.[13]

Flirting is honest appreciation and celebration of our humanness. Don't manipulate. Don't be aggressive. Just flirt. It's a chance to connect to each other because we want to be noticed.

While waiting for my roommate at a café, a young man of about my age initiated a conversation with me.

"I really love your shirt."

I looked up from my novel and then back down to my shirt. "Oh! Thanks!" I responded, looking back up at him.

"What's the label?" He asked.

I smiled, "It's from Express…But, I actually found it for three dollars at a thrift store."

The conspiratorial smiles he tossed me over the lid of his laptop, led me to believe he was coming on to me. But who was I to dash the hope of this young man? And, honestly, there weren't a lot of guys excited about the rewards of treasure hunting in a thrift store's men's section, so why not enjoy the attention and conversation?

In *Flirting 101*, the book from my mystery dinner theatre adventure, Lewis and Bryant assert that, when done right, both parties feel energized and flattered, *and* there's enough ambiguity so that either party can walk away without hurt feelings.[14] We finished our conversation and I returned to my book; though we continued to chat on and off.

He looked as if he was considering advancing the conversation, which would doubtlessly lead to my having to explain that I was simply flamboyantly straight. He was, however, halted in his considerations when the little bell at the door chimed, and into the café walks my roommate, Dan. Fresh from his haircut, sporting a leather jacket and sailor stripped polo; he looked good and he knew it. Our obviously familiar greeting was enough to give my flirting partner pause. And if it wasn't, there was also the fact that I immediately handed him my drink to taste. That (un)timely entrance did two things. First, it implicitly confirms my homosexuality, which at least assuages his ego as it pertains to "gaydar." So, point for him…even though it's wrong. Second, the hope-dashing, not awesome, but a supremely convenient exit strategy. Everyone was able to walk away with dignity.

I've been the flirt initiator and the flirt reciprocator. So, when it's done correctly, flirting is a boon for all parties involved. But, don't take my word for it. A wealth of good stuff has been written on the subject of flirting. A lot of crappy stuff has been written, too. Flirting is definitely a topic worth doing some reading on. Try not to throw the baby out with the bathwater. If you're interested in doing some reading on your own, here a few of the titles I've enjoyed:

–*The Flirting Bible* by **Fran Greene**[15]

–*Flirting 101: How to Charm Your Way to Love, Friendship, and Success*
by **Michelle Lia Lewis and Andrew Bryant**[16]

–*Why Men Don't Have a Clue and Women Always Need More Shoes*
by **Barbara and Allan Pease**[17]

–*Superflirt* by **Tracey Cox**[18]

–*How to Talk to Girls* by **Alec Greven**[19]

R.D.T.

Let me start by saying I'm on a campaign against
D.T.R. Not that I think that people shouldn't take the
time to add some definition to the awkward,
amorphous, hangout fest that is early relational life.
Just don't call it a "Define the Relationship." It's not
nounal phrase and sounds ignorant when being
treated as a noun, "We had a D.T.R." or "I usually
avoid the D.T.R. before the third date." We had a
define the relationship?!? When I hear that, I feel the
same as when I hear, "Git 'er done," which translates
to, "Do her," and makes me throw up in my mouth a
little. I do admit that D.T.R. comes connotatively
closer to its meaning than "Git 'er done," but I can't
help judging it. At the very least, it could be the
"D.T.R. Talk." That way it becomes, "We had a
defining the relationship talk," or a "D.T.R. Talk," or a
"D.T.R.T.," if you're really addicted to acronyms.

But now, I'm endorsing a new candidate for this little
piece of nomenclature: R,D,T. Relationship-Defining
Talk, an actual nounal phrase that can accurately be
used as such. You can now officially use a tightly
constructed three-lettered acronym with all the same
letters as its illegitimate predecessor in its
grammatically-correct form. Once R.D.T. catches on,
people can actually go from "It's complicated," to

dating (a.k.a. It's complicated) without sounding like
E.S.L. dropouts.

Of course, I realize that I'm probably tilting at
windmills and should allow language to evolve as it
sees fit. Nevertheless, I've always fought losing battles
when it comes to language. When you contract the
word, "until" the resultant word is " 'til" not "till"
which is its own word, and probably wants to be
recognized as such. I also rally for the proper usage of
the words "further" and "farther." And, the hole-filled
bowl used to rinse veggies and pasta is a colander, not
a strainer. And, peruse means, "to read thoroughly,"
not "to skim." So, when I take up the cause of the
R.D.T. I know I'm in for a long battle with little hope
for victory.

Nonetheless, Relationship-Defining-Talks are
essential and complicated. So, here are a few things to
keep in mind and/or bring up when your next R.D.T.
rolls around.

When trying to initiate an R.D.T., deepen your voice to
its most resonant tone and say, "We need to talk."
Your attempt to clarify the relationship will be further
aided by inserting uncharacteristically long pauses
between words, in a way which inspires the ominous
dun…Dun…DUNNN!!! At the end.

At the outset, try to establish a grossly disparate
power distribution. Your chair should sit five to ten
inches above your opponent… I mean partner. If
possible, make their chair less comfortable. In the
event they try to stand or change chairs, squirm
uncomfortably in your chair and sigh a lot, while
explaining that their change intimidates you and

makes it harder for you to engage in such a sensitive conversation under those circumstances when it seems like they're trying to gain the upper hand. If they point out your higher, more comfortable position, explain that previous RDTs have left you feeling manipulated... And, you already experience a slight inequality of power, not significant enough to mention, but noticeable.

When your partner tries to mention things that are particularly important, nod your head super-fast and give the "move it along" gesture. If they break to collect their thoughts or take a breath, jump in with the idea (s)he reminded you of while they were nattering on.

Increase the emotional intensity of the discussion every time there's a shift in the conversation. This can be achieved in a number of ways. Moving abruptly to a more sensitive topic, talking louder, and gesticulating more and more broadly are just a few of the ways to achieve that effect.

Some important things to cover during the RDT:

Does your potential partner load the toilet paper so that the new sheet comes over the roll or... the wrong way?
 Digital vs. Analog?
North Face or Columbia?
Tomatoes: evil or just nasty?
NCIS or CSI?
Wolverines or Buckeyes?
Mac or Windows...or Linux?

As soon as you feel like you've covered enough in your RDT, or if you're bored, stand up; pat your partner on the head, and leave.

If you have the time and the resources, follow in the footsteps of Dr. Sheldon Cooper, and consider drafting a "Relationship Agreement."[20] Here are some Cooper-inspired clauses to include:

Retain unilateral control of the thermostat.
When showering second, enough hot water must remain for your morning ritual.
Maintain veto power over all non-headphone audio in the residence and vehicles.
You should probably have a more than equal say on the household television viewing lineup.

So, now you have the tools you need to have a quality Relationship-Defining Talk, *assuming that your primary goal is never to have a relationship among peers.* Even my worst RDT didn't look like this one, though it was definitely problematic. On the one hand, it was a conversation between peers, full of mutual respect and honest consideration of real issues; while on the other, it took place in a stairwell of a campus apartment. And, when it was ultimately defined, it was the relationship of friends—not what she was hoping for.

My RDT Experiences

One of my RDTs went from 11:00 p.m. to 6:30 a.m....on the morning I had an eight-page paper due.

Another was sitting on an ultimate Frisbee field.

Then there was the one over the phone, which was not my finest work, but I was in high school.

The most memorable RDT occurred in a Wal-Mart in the middle of the night. It sucked because the girl was moving out of state. But then again, it rocked because we decided to take the long distance route which led us to getting married!

Relationships are all unique. Therefore, your RDT probably won't look exactly like any of mine. Just make sure you keep it respectful. Have an agenda, but don't be inflexible. Remember, you're having the RDT because you care. Don't lose sight of that when digging around the mechanics of the relationship.

Good Luck.

Ten Things I Think You Should Know

Most guys joke that women should come with an instruction manual. The problem with a manual on women is that most guys who should read it, won't. So here are some of the things I tried and sometimes erred on in my quest to be a better guy. Most of it, you've seen, read, or heard before, but from what I've seen, these things bear repeating. Others are completely personal tips and bits of experience I've garnered through life episodes. The suggestions here can be influential. Do not take them lightly. They are intended to be used by men, or the masculine partner, with a woman or the feminine partner, who are seriously intending to improve a long term relationship. If you use these tips for any other ploy, trick, scam, or whatever, the Universe will convulse and drop a monstrous batch of... karma on you.

I. Everyone wants to be loved for what's on the inside, but knowing that you appreciate what's on the outside boosts your partner's self-esteem in a special way. A picture is worth exceedingly more than a thousand words. Watching you as you observe her builds her confidence in your admiration for her. Three particular photos may serve you well in that endeavor. You may not want them all, but they've each got value.

a. Get a print of you and her. Frame it. Make it prominent. It should be visible within a short distance of the entrance to your space, house, apartment, or room (if you have roommates without much useful shared space). It should be a brightly lit shot, not more than half a body, ideally a head shot ending around the shoulders.

b. Grab a nice shot of her alone. Ask her to provide you with the picture so that a) she knows it exists and b) it's a picture that SHE is confident about. It should also be printed. This one goes in your room, also in a frame. Keep it visible, but it doesn't have to be on a display like Option A.

c. The third photo I recommend is THE action shot; one which showcases an adventure or event. This one comes with you wherever you go. It could be printed or on your phone. It could be her or both of you, but no one else. It's only important that you have an excuse to show it often, preferably a story that's not too mind numbing. Make it happen.

II. Do something ordinary. Awesomely, a personal favorite of mine was having a picnic with my girlfriend in my living room. It was nice, because it was easier to create a romantic vibe. A cheese tray, a basket of fruit, and a bunch of flowers went a long way. But I was free to pan sear scallops for the picnic as well. Another set of options: You love sports. She loves kids. Take her to a little league game. And if you can swing it, go to a game from her hometown or school. Bring coloring pages to the restaurant with you and have a coloring contest. Let the server judge it and figure out a prize of some kind. Another great suggestion for the baller on a budget is to decorate your house according to a theme and have a friend serve as your waiter for the evening.

Dan had been seeing this girl, Gillian, from work for a few weeks and realized that there should be some sort of relational definition. Dan tends to be direct. Sometimes, it comes off as efficient. Other times it comes off as abrasive and alienating. Therefore, he was a little worried as to how his version of the relationship defining talk would go. So, we brainstormed a little bit, and tried to find a way to merge his directness with the overall positive nature of the conversation. If we were lucky, maybe it would come off as playfulness.

Sometimes you have to bring youth into your adulthood. So on their date at Panera Bread, when Gillian sat down, Dan slid a note across the table to her—a classic move straight out of junior high. "Will you be by girlfriend? Yes [ ] No [ ]." On the reverse side, it said, "Are you sure?!"

She still has the note. And, they still have each other. Something so simple...so ordinary...so perfect.

III. Create or commission something about her or for her. A poem, a story, a painting, a drawing, or a song are all nice possible gestures. You want it to exist permanently, and be referenced for reasons greater than practicality or function. When my then-girlfriend was moving six hours and a state line away, I created a six-hour music compilation of significant music pieces from throughout my life, childhood to the present. It was fun, and she still listens to it regularly. But, she took my gift and improved upon it. Using an audio editor, she cut key lines from many of the songs and combined them into a custom tailored re-mix. It makes me smile, every time.

IV. Pet peeves are universal. You have a deep hatred of something that doesn't really warrant it. Your girlfriend has a thing she hates, too. It's totally irrational. And guess what? You don't even know what it is. You know how a wisp of dense smoke slowly creeps up after you blow out a candle? One of my best friends and closest advisors absolutely hates the smell of said candle smoke, it bothers her to no end. Would you be willing to be her knight in shining armor and lick your two fingers to stop the smoke? By the same token, my wife loathes pineapple. Her distaste for pineapple is so strong that when I mentioned grapefruit, she spewed minutes of vitriol before realizing that I didn't say pineapple. Needless to say, I don't bring any pineapple-flavored products into the house.

V. Chivalry is a difficult concept to nail down. It denotes a long-dead code of conduct from ancient knighthood, which includes the instruction, "Show no mercy to the Infidel. Do not hesitate to make war with them." It connotes something, completely different, and a little bit amorphous. Chivalry gets jostled around from camp to camp depending on the speaker. It can come off as arrogant and demeaning or charming and thoughtful. So really, you just have to figure out what works for you. You don't want to come off as trying too hard or misogynistic. Whether you are acquaintances, friends, or romantic partners, it all depends on you. My suggestion is stick to these two classics. Extend your arm, and open her door. When you're walking with your partner, stick your arm out in a way that recalls European High society. It looks cool. And your girlfriend's friends will think it's lovely. In the same vein, open the door for her. Don't happen to be walking in front of her and grab the door. It's worth it to do the awkward double-time step to beat her to the door and hold it open while she walks in, before you. And although my sources tell me that getting out of the car is less important, when you're getting INTO the car, every now and then, make sure you open her door. It just might lead to opening other *doors* for you.

VI & VII. I love the 2005 movie Hitch. It's not that it's a brilliant piece of cinema, though it is a good one. It is a decent primer on navigating the dating realm. There are enough nuggets of wisdom provided to up the regular guy's game. Counseling one of his clients Hitch says,

...And when she answers, don't be looking at her mouth. Don't be wondering what she looks like naked. Listen to what she is saying and respond. Listen and respond. That way, when it's your turn to talk...you'll have something better to say than, "I like your mouth."[21]

If you are like most men, you have a talent for compartmentalizing your thoughts and concerns. You can keep work at work, etc. You also use language to problem-solve or to make linguistic power moves. If you're in any kind of romantic partnership, however, your partner is unlikely to share that trait. Much of the psycho-social research available indicates that— for women—speech serves a number of functions including organization, coping, and relational maintenance. So, as far as guidance is concerned, listening and responding could have been numbers one through ten. We'll tuck them right in the middle and add some specific suggestions.

VI. Listen. In their book, *Why Men Don't Listen and Women Can't Read Maps*, Barbara and Allan Pease

discuss women's use of speaking.[22] "A woman uses
words to show participation and build relationships,
and so, for her, words are a kind of reward. If she likes
you, is buying what you are saying, or wants to be
your friend, she talks to you a lot." So you have to be
prepared to listen. Take a chunk of time out of each
day to just listen to your partner, some days she might
need every second you've allotted, some days she
won't. But listening regularly will go a long way. And
if you're inspired, take an hour or so out of your busy
week and just converse.

VII. Respond. If you are anything like me, you
struggle with the second half of the conversational
contract, which can be even trickier than sitting still
for 20 minutes. Fundamentally, men are hardwired to
solve problems. We love being faced with an
interesting problem that falls within our skill set.
Deborah Tannen, Ph.D., taught us that the
opportunity to demonstrate our prowess and improve
our social standing is a prized event for many men.[23]
Men will discuss almost anything before their own
problems. Because exposing your issues opens them to
the bros for solving. And in a guy mind, the solver has
magic powers over the man who had the problem.
That's why you won't ask for directions or read the
instructions. Who wants a stranger to have magic
power over them?

When you're talking with a woman, on the other hand,
there is usually no expectation or desire for the
listener to solve the problem at hand. Using
unfocused, indirect talk is just a way for many women
to develop a rapport with the listener. You have to
understand that there will likely be no agenda. To
respond effectively, you can try using listening sounds

and body language, to demonstrate visually and aurally. Repeating or rephrasing things you've just heard are also effective responses. If your desire to contribute runs a bit deeper, ask if there's anything you could do to help her deal with this particular issue. And I hope this one is obvious, answer questions she asks.

I've not always been amazing at these things, sometimes the problem solver gets the best of me; and I cut her off mid thought. Other times I drift off and fail to respond when called upon, but as a general rule, I'm told I do a good job. The fact that I "conversationally engage effectively" is one of my best qualities, according to a dear friend of mine. One last bit of advice regarding your convo time. Turn off your phone. Duty will still be calling when your conversation is over. There is a massive amount of value hidden in conversation. Dig.

VIII. Shut Up and Think. We just discussed talking, and now I'm recommending clamming up. It doesn't seem fair, but fairness doesn't appear often in nature; it appears even less in relationships. Solomon wrote, "Even a fool, when he keeps silent, is considered wise; When he closes his lips, he is *considered* prudent" (Proverbs 17:28).[24] Another great quote, with slightly more murky provenance includes, "It's better to keep your mouth shut and appear stupid than open it and remove all doubt." Sometimes sharing the stream of conscious thoughts with your partner will be a wonderful tool in developing your relationship. At other times, you might want to take a breath and reflect on a few things. In a given day, a lot of things will pop into your head. Things which, with your peers or friends, would be totally okay to say, but wouldn't really help your relational growth. Consider whether or not this thing you want to mention, is worth fighting over? And, if it is; is it a hill worth dying on? Thirty seconds of awkward silence is greatly preferable to three hours of fighting (unless you have a safe bet on make-up sex).

IX. When it comes to emotional investment and relational development, Barnabus Stinson isn't exactly a role model. This womanizing know-it-all from TV's *How I Met Your Mother* has a rule and a lesson for everything. Most of his rules are misogynistic, some are absurd, and some are dangerous. There is one area in which it's okay to follow in his custom-made shoe-shaped footsteps; his style. In their very first meeting, he offers to teach Ted how to live. And, while I don't think that a goatee absolutely doesn't go with your suit. I'm absolutely on board with lesson two, "Get a suit. Suits are cool." In the episode *Singles Stamina,* Barney lectures his brother on their way of life, "Do you remember why we suit up, James? [...]To show people that we are different from the millions of T-shirt and jeans lemmings out there. The suit shows that we are a force to be reckoned with, a two-person army that plays by its own rules."[25]

You don't have to suit up every time, but every so often, you have to take it up a notch. More frequently, though, a button-down shirt with full-length sleeves, a pair of dress trousers, and an honest to goodness tie are your uniform for the night. If you look special, she feels special. She can take you out with pride, instead of buyer's remorse. So button your shirt, all the way to the top (no faking). Dust off/Salvo/borrow a tie. Sorry,

no polos or jeans allowed. Shy away from khakis even,
unless you really know how to dress them up.
For a value boost, get a professional haircut. And let
your significant other or someone more fashion savvy
than you create your ensemble. [The author is
available for a reasonable fee.]

X. God is in the details.
The same way that protecting her from the little
things she hates is important, it's a million tiny things
that make you the boyfriend that she talks about with
her friends. Brush her hair away when it falls into her
eyes. Carry an umbrella that you hold over her when
it rains. Slip a hair tie in your briefcase, sometimes
she'll need it. Write "thinking of you" on a post-it and
stick it in her glove box or the bottom of her laptop or
inside her jacket pocket. You've heard that it's the
little things…I'm telling you, it's true.

Delusion: A Cautionary Tale

So, I am, admittedly, not exactly fair and balanced when it comes to relational analyses. As mentioned before, my best friends are mostly women. And, after being the shoulder to cry on for one too many bad breakups, it's easy to see the male population as being evil (not exactly the most self-serving position, but truthful), and women as being made of sugar, spice, etc. Anyway, as a way of bringing a touch of balance to this work, we will have a short segment on the dark side of girlhood. A special thanks to my wife Jessica for helping to bring this piece to life.

<u>Girls: The B Side</u>
Girls are sometimes characterized as truly and generally pleasant beings on this earth. However, they can also be manipulative, evil sprites who take control and get away with everything. Let us go through the high school dating process.

Attraction or How Girls Manipulate Guys: A girl, let's call her Lucia gets all dressed up for school with her short skirt and low-cut shirt to get some poor, unassuming guy's attention, we'll call him Seth. Once there, she will walk around flaunting everything that she has (or lacks). When she runs into Seth accidentally on purpose, she makes eye contact, flutters her eyelashes, and does a well-practiced "hair flip." After getting his attention a few times, she casually starts a conversation with him. When the dust settles, Seth has a date on Friday and no idea what just happened.

Preparation: If Seth arrives at the prescribed time, Lucia may only be in the first hour of getting ready. First, she has to shower, which can take more than twenty minutes by itself because she must shave, wash, and do her hair. Then, she has to get dressed. This can take some additional hours because she can get lost in her closet, which some might say is equivalent to being lost in the jungle. It's not that she didn't pick out an outfit the day he asked her out. She has selected and re-selected her outfit a few times each day since then. "I have nothing to wear!" is a common statement made by one who has two closets for her dress clothes, a dresser for casual clothes, and a whole other closet just for her shoes. But, eventually she'll settle on a passable outfit. Now the real work begins; her hair and make-up. For the sake of time and mystery, we'll skip that step.

Foraging: By the time she is ready to walk out the door, her date is sleeping and she says, "Aren't you ready? We have to get going," fully aware that her date had been waiting for two and half hours for her to be ready.

In his enthusiasm, he scurries behind the wheel, as she stares disdainfully at the handle, waiting for him to open the car door for her. As he hustles back around to her side of the car, the conversation begins:

Seth: Where would you like to eat this evening?

Lucia: [*Smiling thinly*] I don't care. You choose.

Seth: How about [Mexican restaurant]?

Lucia: Ooo, I don't like Mexican.

Seth: How about [American restaurant]?

Lucia: That place has terrible service.

Seth: How about [Italian restaurant]?

Lucia: Are you serious? You like that place?

Seth: ...

Now he's stuck because he really does like that restaurant, but does not want to look dumb in front of her. So he offers more restaurants, and finally asks her again where she wants to go. She still tells him, "I don't care." Finally, after twenty minutes of blind guessing, Seth picks the correct restaurant, and they're off...

Dining: They walk into the restaurant, and she sees her Rival, Viola. Viola is the girl who likes Seth and has been after him for some time, but was too slow to sink her talons into him. *I got him first*, Lucia thinks. But then doubt sets in, *Maybe, we should just leave. I don't want her to steal my trophy.* Instead, she decides to make Viola jealous. As Lucia and Viola lock eyes, Lucia latches onto Seth's arm. Once in their booth, she sits next to him so they can make-out if she really needs to give the right impression. This game continues throughout the evening, giving Seth the impression that he has it made. In her mind, the date is just a battleground. *Good*, she thinks, *Viola knows that this is my man, and she can't have him.*

The Return: At the end of the evening, Seth drives her home thinking he will definitely score the goodnight kiss. Lucia again tries to will him to open the door. Instead, he leans over and tries to kiss her. Horrified, she bolts from the car, slamming the door in his face. Dazed and confused Seth stumbles out of the car and into the line of fire. "What kind of girl do you think I am?!?" Her indignant glare chills him to the core, "Do you think I'd make-out on the first date?" He does not know how to respond and stares puzzled, *She was all over me at the restaurant...all I wanted to do was kiss her goodnight.* She stomps off, not believing what just happened. What would make him think she's that kind of girl?

The Aftermath: The next day at school, she catches Viola with Seth (He figured there was no chance of a second date so, whatever). Lucia walks over to Viola and begins to reassert her claim on Seth, provoking an argument. He tries to protest saying that he is not anyone's, but in the string of bad language and big attitudes, there's not a lot of room for his opinion. Seth leaves unnoticed, and the girls continue until the bell rings. Viola and Lucia part ways, plotting escalation.

It's Never the End

Girls can be catty, hold grudges, and torment one another in subtle and treacherous ways. While guys duke it out and it is over, girls scheme and try to get back at one another evilly. This grudge match from the story went on for weeks. A perfect example of a well-executed coup comes straight out of the annals of

Newbury High School. In a scenario not unlike the preceding, "Lucia" bought a red slushy and dumped it on "Viola's" white clothing; a particularly cruel revenge because of its propensity to stain and the added insult of looking like a most unfortunate, accident of menstruation. The final salvos of the actual conflict all occurred despite the fact that "Seth" had moved on and was totally out of the picture.

It seems that pairs of high school girls, when sent to the office, act like angels and pretend nothing at all is happening, avoiding any real backlash from the principal or counselor. After all of that is finished, they go back to war, until they finally realize that another girl has "stolen" the Seth. Insta-truce! Viola and Lucia become best friends. Now it's time to team up on the other girl. She is now the enemy.

The games girls play are like a never ending suspense movie. One moment they are pleasant and genial; the next minute they are behind someone, creeping up on them to stab them in the back. Girls are like cats, prowling around waiting for the perfect opportunity to attack. They rub up against someone's leg and pretend they need someone to care for them, but then they hiss and attack with their extended claws.

Perhaps this characterization swings far in the other direction, but I did chuckle the day she showed this piece of fictitious criticism. I figured I should share it with you.

Staying Attached:
Hand Holding

Hand holding is one of the basic components of romance. It rates so low on the scale of affectionate contact that it doesn't get a base. It would be the baseline on the way to "kissing?" It's a little odd how that works. It's hard to build a relationship without it. But it doesn't show up nearly as often in established relationships. Anyway, as a consummate people watcher I get to see couples hand in hand all over. During undergrad, there was a couple who was almost famous for their method of clasping. The duo even had a nickname based on their technique, "the 90-degree couple." Try to imagine with me, two people standing approximately two feet apart, separated by almost the exact distance of their collective shoulder-to-elbow span. Because, they're standing scarecrow style, forearms dangling into a grip knot of fingers, suspended over the sidewalk. Tragic.

Hand holding is a pretty nice thing. It's an element of closeness available when other such demonstrations of affection aren't appropriate. It's a promise of something enduring. Palms of each partner nestled in the hand of the other. Or for the more intimate, there is the passionate intertwining of fingers. Hand holding is a desire to cherish each other despite engaging in extraneous activities (walking, TV watching, or even writing). It's connection despite "whatever." And it communicates so much to each partner and to the rest of the world.

Is hand holding her leash, whereby she can drag her reticent partner from store to store at the mall? Or a pacifier to silence her during the game? Trying not to lose him in a crowd? Is it a tangible, "I love you?" Or did you just forget that the "Red Rover" game ended.

In another category, there is the hyper-jealous partner. Not like typical jealous ("No, you can't go out alone with your ex"). Or even very jealous ("Was that guy checkin' you out"). But, he's the kind of guy whose jealous insecurity oozes out of all of his body language, interposing himself between his hostage... I mean, partner, and the person foolish enough to step in between him and the object of his possession. The dead giveaway is when you see the happy couple charging down the street holding hands. But, holding hands is a terribly flawed way to describe the activity. As opposed to the fingers being lovingly intertwined, or even each hand tucked neatly between the thumb and the forefinger, he's got her in "The Clamp." His hand encases her entire hand, thumb included, in a vice grip of possession. Someday, they'll realize that he doesn't own her.

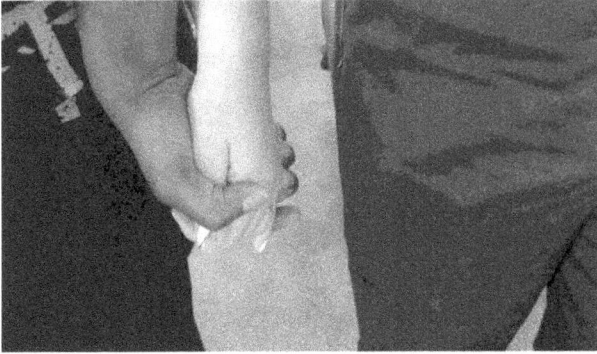

Like I said already, hand holding is a funny thing. It's an electric shock through your body, the first time that it happens. But when the novelty wears off, people forget that it's about connecting to your partner. So whether you've been dating for two weeks or married for two decades, take your partner's hand, and try a little tenderness. But don't be vice grip guy.

May I Propose

The following is a case study of sorts. It features the story of a young man who pays attention like very few men I've ever known. In this one story, he successfully incorporated elements I, II, III, and X, from the *Ten Things I Think You Should Know* list, for those of us who wish to take a step toward exceptional.

My dear friend Tess, an art teacher with whom I went to school, had been seeing Brandon, a nice enough young man (even though they're never really good enough for your "dear friends"), for something like three years. Living in the hills of central Pennsylvania (a redundancy, I know), they were prone to picturesque walks. On one such walk, along a trail, Tess saw another classmate of ours, Greg, a fellow artist. "What a crazy coincidence," she asserts.

"Not at all," Brandon replied. "I asked Greg here, to paint a portrait of us in the park."

So, they set up in a cute little hand-holding pose, and Greg gets to work—sketch, sketch, sketch, paint, paint, paint. Bam! Done. He turns the painting around for the subjects to admire.

"Wow, this is incredible. Brandon, this was so thoughtful. Wait...I don't have a ring?" Greg takes the painting. And Brandon takes a knee and asks Tess to be his...forever.

I'd say that he understands that God is in the details.

Alone Together

As they sat, eyes fixed on their matching his & hers
iPod covers, ear buds dangling into their laps, they
glanced up occasionally, briefly taking in snatches of
the outside and of each other.

Brow furrowed, his eyes rarely left his music player,
turned digital organizer. Not looking up as he sipped
from his coffee cup, his work is his only aim.

Legs crossed, foot waving, her glances are frequent
and erratic, looking for interest, and to be interesting.
She is amused to see the twenty-something near the
window scratching away at his pad. She wonders what
he's writing about; and smiles to herself, as she
wonders if he knows how much there is to learn, that
he can't possibly know... yet.

The Best Friend Myth

When we got married, my wife and I promised not to go to bed angry.
I haven't slept since Wednesday.

I love her. But, she does not complete me, and there is no second pea in my pod. I don't have an adjoining puzzle piece, another half, a better half, a worse half or any other comparable component finishing the person I am. I have a wife. I was a complete person before we met, and so was she. I like *Doctor Who* and *The Office*. I read as much as I can everywhere I go. She reads what Needs to be read... or is interesting. I am a gut reactor. She's a logistics queen. I try to keep worrying to a minimum...I'm pretty sure she does, too, but her minimum is a lot higher than mine. That isn't to say we haven't each grown as individuals because of the other's influence. But, I am a person, and so is she. We each have strengths and weaknesses. We each have friends and enemies. We each have likes and dislikes. Some of those things we share. Others remain in the other's life alone.

I have a great best friend. We've known each other since nursery, were friends through childhood, and became the best of friends during our time together in college.

I've gone days and weeks without talking to my best friend. Then we just catch up. My best friend knows every girl I've ever dated. My best friend and I feel obligated to...nothing.

But, I've told my best friend about every crush I've ever had. I've behaved like an ass with my best friend. When my best friend and I disagree on anything that's not totally fundamental to our friendship, we discuss it, and then drop it, never to retrieve it again... unless, it's funny. Nevertheless, we kept each other safe. When I was attracted to an inappropriate girl my best friend told me I was stupid, and I needed to lock that insanity down. Every time I met a girl who was appropriate, my best friend helped me manage my expectations.

When I met the woman I wanted to marry, I called my best friend. The day we said, "I love you," I called my best friend. When the woman I wanted to marry flipped out on me, I called my best friend. When the woman I wanted to marry changed her mind about some pretty major stuff and I needed to scream at someone, I called my best friend. When I needed to mourn the loss of my singleness, I called my best friend. When I was getting excited to propose, I called my best friend. The manic depressive days leading up to my wedding, I called my best friend... a lot.

I married my lover. We've known each other for a few years. It feels like we're exploring life together intimately. Many of our memories, and most of our years are ahead of us, Lord willing. I am a better person with her than without her. And with her, I am becoming a person I never even dreamt I could be. We push through complex areas of disagreement. We try to inspire each other daily. We shop together. Do each other's laundry. Trudge, stroll, saunter, and sprint through life together. My life, in a very real sense, revolves around my wife's. And, hers around mine.

Maybe your lover is your best friend. But, calling my wife my best friend would do a disservice to my wife and to my best friend. Some problems require a deeply trusted external set of eyes. When you find yourself struggling with temptation or relational angst, your best friend knows your history, your mind, and your motivation. That friend has comparatively little emotional investment in the relationship, and can help you with your issues without ever feeling attacked, dismissed, or slighted. My best friend is my on-deck circle for other life issues. I can work the kinks out of my home run swing, before I actually take a shot at the fence. If I devolve into a stream of consciousness, there's very little chance my best friend will burst into tears. There is, history would indicate, a one in three chance that my wife will. But, if I've worked a little bit of the cognitive tension out earlier with my best friend, I'm less likely to strike out altogether, and much more likely to work through the big issue in question.

Nonetheless, when the world is weighing on you day after day, your partner, your lover, your significant other keeps picking up the pieces and putting you back together.

The strength of a web is that if one part is compromised, the other parts redistribute that part of the burden. If you're entire emotional support group consists of a single person, that person has to always be on standby. That's a lot of undue, unhealthy pressure. I take my sanity where I can get it. Thankfully, between my wife, and my body of friends, I have a very good pool of support.

Playing the Field for Charity

February is the month that kills the casual
relationship. It doesn't matter if you've been seeing
each other for two weeks or eleven months, round
about the ides of February, casual dating comes to a
screeching halt. You have to scale your number of
dating partners down to one. And that one is your
girlfriend...or you're single.

Every Valentine's Day, guys are faced with the choice
to spend quality time with one specific girl on that
day, after which everything changes. You can't go out
with one girl on the 14th and then tell her you can't see
her the next day because you're seeing some other girl.
And, let's be honest, the girl you didn't see on
Valentine's, probably doesn't want to talk to you
anyway. So, yeah, Cupid's bow is a kill shot for dating
more than one woman. I don't mean to say it's
impossible to continue casually dating a few women

through the barrier that is February fourteenth. It just requires a degree of cunning and calculation.

Our junior year of college a few of us are sitting around the table and the conversation swings to everyone's plan for Valentine's Day. This for my friend, Brian, means the "two-girl conundrum."

"You know how you're stringing two chicks along, 'cause they're both cool, but you're not sure whom you like more," Brian begins. "Valentine's Day ruins everything. The girl you don't take out hates you. And, the girl you take out is automatically your girlfriend. It really sucks."

One of our tablemates piped up, "Wow Brian, that's so romantic. And by, 'so romantic,' I mean, you might be a monster."

"Stay with me," Brian reasserted, "Dating casually, allows people to get to know each other one on one, but leaves out the looming specter of a big break up or too much weight being placed on either party in the relationship. It gives confused young people, such as us, a chance to just see where something is going.

"And, regardless, Valentine's Day is a hyper-inflated, commercialized monstrosity of a holiday. It's a way for Hallmark to gouge America one more time before the Easter/ Mother's Day/Father's Day season begins..." This highly amusing, disturbingly well thought out diatribe goes on for another five or so minutes.

Here's the thing about Brian. In addition to sometimes displaying all of the charming indicators of complete sociopathology, he is one of the smartest people I know. He staggers into more great ideas than a think tank. So, as he finishes extolling the virtue of casually dating a few people at a time and decrying the cruelty of choosing on Valentine's Day, he gets that look.

"Really you need a way to not to take either girl out on Valentine's and have them both be okay with it. You could probably score some points by taking out a mentally handicapped girl…or an old lady. If you took a grandma out on Valentine's day, you'd score a ton of points."

"Brian, you still sound like a monster."

But less than a week later I get a call from Brian who has reached out to the college administration and the activities coordinator from a local retirement community. Sixteen of us are going to take residents out to dinner on Valentine's Day.

The big day arrives. We pick the ladies up at the main building. We give them roses. We go out to a restaurant. We talk. We have a fabulous time. And, we come home. Brian, for his part, makes it through a Valentine's Day without hurting anyone's feeling or committing.

There was a great deal said and written about the events of Valentine's Day 2005. The school paper and the alumni magazine both did feature pieces on our little outing. The college received a bunch of great free publicity, including a write-up with pictures on the front of the local section of the Harrisburg newspaper. Brian was quoted as saying, "We were all together around the table in the cafeteria talking about what everyone was doing for Valentine's Day, trying to come up with alternate things we could do." And, while I suppose that's one way of saying it, the other way is, "I really wanted to keep my options open."

So if February rolls around, and you happen to be casually dating a few women, consider starting a charity outreach program. You can improve your overall standing and keep from pissing off your non-girlfriends.

Fun as a Plus One

In between girlfriends, going out is still fun. The three "D"s—dinner, dancing, and drinks—are no less exciting because you're not seeing someone. In fact, they can be more fun.

Long before Vince Vaughn and Owen Wilson taught us that anyone can have a bright future working at Google, they showed us that going to weddings can be lots of fun. Of course, they mostly used the weddings as a means to get laid. But still, they had a lot of fun at the wedding itself.[26] Going to weddings when you don't know many or any people is a completely different kind of fun. While I never signed on to the whole wedding crasher plan, I did a stint on the "plus one" circuit, and I had a spectacular time.

As I have enjoyed arm-candy status, you can too. Here are a few things I did which may serve you well:

Be well maintained—women don't want to have to strain their brain muscles to imagine you in a suit. Give your female friends an inkling you clean up well. This is a fairly easy image to create. Shaving should not be a special occasion; shave regularly. And by regularly, I mean three to four times per week. If you have facial hair, choose a style and maintain it. Don't always wear the same outfit and don't wear heinously worn out clothing.

Be self-contained—have you ever gone to a party and seen the guy who needs his date? He stands inches away from her the entire night looking bored whenever she isn't explicitly including him in the conversation or activity. Don't be that guy, ever. Be the person who steps away and introduces himself to the other guests or looks at the exhibits. Participate in the activities, as appropriate, and watch, politely engaged, when it's not.

Learn to dance—two or three lessons at the YMCA will give you enough of a primer to make you stand out in any typical reception. Dance a few dances with your *date*, throw in a dance with the flower girl, and then you can usually sneak a few dances in with various other unaccompanied female attendees. Don't forget to circle regularly back to the person who invited you.

Prepare to be her wingman—she invited you, but you're not on a date. If something comes up, be ready to roll with the waves. If you see a guy trying to talk to her, be complimentary, and if she seems to like his attention, be invisible. Hang at the periphery. Go back to chatting with the guests you charmed back in point two. Be ready to step in if she needs it, but don't hover anxiously.

Have fun—being a plus one means being invited to a wedding where you are free to be anyone. Weddings are fun in general. It's even more fun to be at a wedding where no one knows the stupid things you did in elementary school or middle school or high school or college or grad school or the office Christmas party. They'll know you for three hours, then you'll be, "Charming guy, who came with Abbie, to Rachel's wedding. You know... the dancer."

To A Young Lady I Know

Have you ever washed your hands in a bathroom at the bus
station and they are out of paper towels (that, or they've
gone into hiding with soap) so you look around
frantically for something to dry your hands with and save
you from getting water on the crotch of your jeans, until you
see it—the toilet paper—the kind that is eight cents a roll,
three-sixteenths ply, strung together by half a dozen
vagabond molecules, and your dripping fingers fumble at it,
dissolving half the roll—that is what talking to you feels like.
    -*Josh Lennon*

If You Don't Flirt Back,
It's Sexual Harassment

Body image is a hot-button issue. Magazines often depict hyper-sexualized bodies, re-formed to an absurd and artificial ideal. There is a struggle that exists among members of the different body types. Daggers are slung outward and self-recrimination eats at the individuals. I didn't want to add to the body hype. And since my message has implication across the spectrum of bodies, it made sense to put everyone on the same side against anger, loneliness, and other such ethereal concepts. So here's my deal...or the deal...or one of a host of deals out there to be addressed, as they relate to the getting together of guys and girls.

I'm in a Facebook community called, "If guys like 'curvy' girls then why do all the skinny ones have boyfriends?" Now, being a self-proclaimed lover of curvy women and knowing that I'm by no means, the only one of my kind, this group is an affront to my sensibilities. Not that it exists...but that it needs to. I spoke a bit with the group's creator who expressed personal and observed frustration at what she saw to be a common singleness among the soft, sloping ranks of the curvy.

There's a great scene in the film, *Spanglish*, in which the narrator ruminates on the nature of body image:

American women, I believe actually feel the same as Hispanic women about weight. A desire for the comfort of fullness. And when that desire is suppressed for style, and deprivation allowed to rule, dieting, exercising, American women become afraid of everything associated with being curvaceous, such as wantonness, lustfulness, sex, food, motherhood, all that is best in life.[27]

She makes some interesting points. And I think that she's mostly right. There is a degree of inner comfort in the natural contours of one's body. Internal confidence engenders a high level of self awareness and introspection. People with high self-awareness and introspective natures make excellent partners. Healthy concerns, expressive emotionally, but not co-dependent. So, to all the self-sustained women living in the comfort of fullness; I want to date you.

Here's the rub.

In some way, shape or form, before "happy couple," comes "flirting strangers." There seem to be a phenomenon wherein lots of people don't like to flirt. But, like that group is based on individual experiences, so is this book. Though hopefully, this is more of a call to action, than pure lament. I am an insatiable flirt. Sometimes I even flirt when I don't want to. I do it for fun. I do it for profit. I do it to get places. I do it to kill time. It's pretty fantastic.

But, it should be a lot like a dance. It's give and take. It's compromise. And, while it would be awesome if all women danced like Blackpool Champions. The reality is a lot of women act like they don't even like to dance, much less be in a dance club.

There's much fun to be had in flirting. I don't understand why people don't do it all the time. Work. School. The mall. Even a challenge like the DMV. But even if I'm polite, deferential, respectful, engaging, and my flirt radar is always pinging, it takes two to tango. Rapport building? Chatting up? Flirting? All of this has to start somewhere. A stranger says, "Hi" on the street. The guy who uses the machine near you in the gym nods to you. The smiling cart pusher in the produce aisle. No matter what something becomes in the future, it usually starts as something else in the past. Most experts identify flirting as a means or an end. If I seem a little obsessed, it's because I am. I don't always flirt...Sometimes I sleep.

A few women, in my experience, are on board with the anytime flirt mentality. At the gym, she's the girl who nods back, and may even remove an earbud for a chat. When you ask to sit next to her at Starbucks, she'll eye you up and may or may not offer you the seat. But, you got the once over. And if you're seriously just flirting then that's all you're asking for, a shot.

Before you decide that ALL guys are horrible, that they only date skinny girls, that they only date _____, make sure you are a comfortable with you, and that your flirt radar is fully charged and operational.

A Superhero in Love

Batman is an icon of...well everything.[28] At one point or another, every little boy in America has uttered the words, "I'm Batman!" He's smarter and cooler than pretty much any other superhero on the block. And in the early '90s, he was pretty much the only universal player in the vigilante game. So, I was him. At six, I was the oldest kid in the little neighborhood band we'd assembled. I was a little faster, and believe it or not, a little tougher, than the rest of the kids we played with. So when we were pretending... I got to be Batman. I think the real reason was the hella sweet cape that my grandmother made for me. But that's neither here nor there.

Robin, the alter ego of my good friend Jeremy, and I, the caped crusader, felled one imaginary foe after another during our many quests. We battled from the ends of the earth to our own backyards. Employing clever devices like rubber bands and empty ice cream buckets, we overcame all odds. No one could stand up to us...until one day.

As a twenty-six year old man, I still haven't nailed down the details of infatuation. Subtract a score of years and a life of experience, I didn't even know the game. And there wasn't anything in the utility belt that aided in talking to girls. Not a big deal for the dynamic duo, but Jay had an older sister.

Robin's, I mean Jay's, older sister Kay, and her friend Meg occasionally played with us. However, joining us in our super heroics was completely unprecedented. When they asked to join us, we of course said yes—

Jeremy, because it was his "cool" older sister, and I, because I had a little kid crush on them.

They followed us on our adventure and ultimately to safety. All that remained was the denouement; the daring escape to the Batcave. This is supposed to be the easy part. But, it wasn't. When I opened my mouth to order the girls into the Batmobile, I choked like George W. Bush on pretzels. But, I was Batman! I rallied, looked them in the eyes, and got as far as, "OK," before dissolving into a shy giggle. Even after they spoon fed me the line, "Come on, girls, hop in the car." I couldn't make it through the word, 'girls.' Somehow, I was sure that if I said that, it would be obvious, that I was "in love" with them. I'd be mortified. They'd be indignant. And Jeremy would...well, I don't know how a five-year-old brother reacts when his six-year-old friend is found to be in love with his eight-year-old sister. But, whatever the reaction, I was fairly sure it wouldn't be good.

A Wing and a Player

A meet-cute is a delightful scene in a movie in which two future romantic partners come together for the first time. These scenes usually involve a moderately contrived set of circumstances which set the stage for a lovely ninety-ish minute path to "Happily Ever After"…or the credits. Unfortunately, in a Venn diagram, the intersection of positively timely circumstances, people to whom you may be attracted, people who may find you attractive, and you actually being on your game, is more like a dot than a region. So people have to figure out ways to engineer their own "meet-cutes."

It can be challenging to arrange a connection with a random stranger. So in an attempt to avoid or at least minimize the risk of soul-crushing, depression-inducing rejection, people have given friends and acquaintances the honor of playing the role of wingman.

When I fly wing for someone, I try to be a supporter. When my friend is choking, I vamp for a little, without stealing the spotlight, 'til he gets his feet back under him. Throw in a well-timed, contextually appropriate compliment about my friend. And then, of course, I engage, distract, or entertain friends of the object of my buddy's affections. I just do what needs to be done to help my friend get a shot with the future Mr. or Mrs. Right. In a particularly ambitious move, I got my friend introduced to the dance team member he kept talking about at this one event we attended.

While I lived in Canton and during my time in college, I had a few great wingmen. We would go out, and have a great time chatting with whomever. We complimented each other, and usually we complimented the other party. There was an almost effortless fluidity. Nothing contrived and no scams, we just extemporized.

Beyond my all-star lineup of wingmen, many of my other friends have returned the favor, at one time or another. Some, however, have not. And others are just so mind-bendingly bad at it, that flying solo doesn't look so bad.

When I moved to D.C., I was starting all over. I didn't have a large pool of associates to pull from. I spent a lot of time going out on my own. It wasn't bad. I got a feel for "The District," and managed to meet and to have fun with a decent number of people. Nevertheless, I wanted to start going out with a wingman again.

Dan is a great guy. He's handy, smart, athletic, and honest. However, his personal taste would tend to lean toward sweats, hoodies, and combat boots, none of which ever seem to match. When he felt dressy he would wear black shirts, military surplus combat pants, and those same combat boots. He was definitely ruggedly handsome but he didn't really do much to tilt the balance from rugged to handsome. You'd think that standing next to a guy wearing a mismatched set of sweats would help me from a pure odds perspective, but carrying on long involved conversations with a guy who looks like he has completely given up, doesn't actually serve your cause. So, while he was excellent as a roommate, his utility as a wingman was negligible at best.

Shortly after moving to D.C., however, Dan and I started training as dance instructors. It was awesome. It was a fun job. I was working with my friend. And most importantly, Dan had to dress up everyday for work; so being seen out with him in public was less of a social handicap than normal.

One Saturday evening after finishing up at the studio, we rode back toward our place, and stopped off at Applebee's so that Dan could drink a generous amount of beer and catch the highlights from the University of Michigan's football game.

We settled into Dan's favorite spot, front and center of the biggest sports television in the restaurant. As we sat there, two attractive girls sitting a few seats down scooted a place closer to us, and started chatting us up.

They asked us what we did professionally. They loved that we were dance teachers.

"What's it like being a dance teacher?" they asked.

"Good," Dan murmured barely above the music, without ever taking his eyes off ESPN.

"Sorry ladies, my friend is a huge Wolverine's fan. And, he's a little distracted waiting to see how they performed today."

They were gracious despite his slight "Ha! Ha! Wow... that's... cool." They proceeded to try and include Dan in our three-way conversation, but were quickly rebuffed each time. Finally, in a desperate attempt to engage him closer to his heart, one of the girls blurted out, "Maryland is so much better than the Wolverines!" That got Dan to look away from the screen.

Mentally, I'm pretty sure I sighed so hard that the girls actually heard it. Dan glared over at the two girls. "What?!" he exploded. "O.K. First, let's disregard the fact that you, technically just compared an entire state to a college. If I just assume that you meant to compare The University of Maryland to The University of Michigan, your argument is still absurd. The Wolverines are the winningest football program in college football. The Terps aren't even in the Big Ten Conference..." At that point, he'd built up a head of steam, and it was a few minutes before the now irate Dan even took a breath, after which he dove quickly back into an intimidating stream of statistical data describing the overwhelming greatness that is U of M football.

The two pretty women started to shrink back in fear of never getting another word in edgewise, or even making it out of the restaurant alive. And, I sank back into my seat. Instead of getting to trade laughs with two beautiful women, I was going to get to trade silences with Dan. And what's worse, even though they pulled the pin, they got to leave. I was going to get to hear him rant insanely for the next few weeks.

Repelling willing and interested women while clinging
to irrational wrath aren't traits one generally seeks in
a wingman.

So, even though, as roommates and friends we did
stuff together on a regular basis, I realized that I
would have to look elsewhere for someone to serve as
my full-time wingman.

After another handful of months flying solo, I called
upon my other roommate, Brian, to take a shot at
filling the wingman-shaped hole in my heart.

There is this great little bar/ restaurant/coffee shop in
Adams Morgan called Tryst. People tended to go there
to socialize a bit, so as long as you weren't overbearing
or gross, you could usually find willing flirt buddies.
Sometimes I'd make a guy friend early in the evening,
and we'd wing through the night. This trip was
different. Bri had expressed interest in taking up the
vacated position. We were meeting with a few people
at Tryst and Bri was going to show me his skills.

At this point, I hadn't been teaching dance for a while.
A minor war between the manager of the studio and
the owner resulted in the manager, and all those loyal
to him, being fired or laid off. The manager was right.
The owner was wrong. I was young and loyal. And
suddenly, I was waiting tables. Even though I had a
line on a possible new dance-teaching position, I
hadn't set foot on a dance floor in about four months.

So when Brian introduces me to one of the girls, we
start the getting to know you conversation.

In D.C., every conversation like that has a rhythm. "Greetings," then, "Where are you really from?" "What brought you to 'The District'?" Then, as with countless other conversations of this genre we make our way quickly to, "What do you do?"

If you're on your game, "What do you do?" is the best question in the entire conversation. From that question, you can hit a few of your favorite hobbies, a few of your passions as well as your dreams. Really, you can do a lot with however little you have.

"I'm an out-of-work dance instructor." I respond, casually. And while I fully intend to circle back to the fact that I was more recently waiting tables; I plan to do that on my terms.

Right on cue, her eyes go wide. Just as she's about to ask, "Wow, you teach ballroom dancing?" Brian, my wingman, the guy who has my back, who will always say "yes," pipes up, "Seriously? You haven't even stepped on a dance floor in like, half a year. Do you seriously still think of yourself as a dance instructor?"

"…Umm." I took a beat to compose, and in that moment realized that there is a fairly substantial difference between going out with another guy and having a wingman. This was the former.
After serious deliberation I've decided, I don't give enough credit to disposable wingmen and flying solo. I never found a permanent wingman during my time in "The District." But, everything turned out okay.

The Chase

I believe in pursuit.

Or rather, I should say, that I like the idea of a romantic pursuit. Sometimes, the chase is pure. You like someone who doesn't really know you. You have to figure out a way to make a connection. Or, you love each other, but the timing isn't right. Geographic. Social. Occupational. In contradistinction to the pure chase is the intricate labyrinth of unrequited love.

Mr. Darcy is one of my favorite romantic characters in all of literature. He was in love with a woman who loathed him (under false pretenses, yet she loathed him, nonetheless). By many ways and by many good deeds, he upended her world 'til she could not help but love him. I believe in that.[29]

Unless you're Mr. Darcy, however, there are a few problems with this particular brand of love-based pursuit, aside from restraining orders. Few twenty-first century charmers and would-be suitors are insanely wealthy men capable of changing everything in their lives to solve the problems of the woman and her family. Let's be honest, in today's financial mess, the beau of the moment, is lucky to upend an afternoon and afford a trip to the vet for her puppy. So if, unlike the stoic and grating Mr. Darcy, you don't have unlimited access, you need charm or whatever passes for it these days.

So you find your Elizabeth. She's beautiful, smart, funny, and driven. She's an all around winner. You hang out often. Maybe, too often. She's mentioned that you are the type of guy that she is looking for in a lifetime partner…"looking for" equals "not you." Because, whatever the future looks like in your imagination, it's the present that is lacking. She likes you; but not in that way. No infatuation and no passion. No fire means, no date.

All that preface, to ask this question to myself and to the universe. You, the reader, being the official representative of the universe, at this time:

Can you "win" someone's heart?

Like most philosophical areas, I have a moderate lean. And when it comes to emotional predestination, I definitely hedge my bets. The chase can be the last step on the road to crazy. But I do believe that time and effort can, sometimes, result in a "happy middle" ("happy endings" usually, being more of a new beginning than an actual end). I interviewed a lady whose suitor trekked from coast to coast missing her by weeks, in one state after another, until he found her. And, they've been married for years now.

My husband and I were high school sweethearts. And during that time my mom was battling stage-four cancer. And so we ended up being split apart before we could even break up with each other. And we moved away, my family and I. And my mom ended up passing away, when I was sixteen (from cancer). And I, kinda just went on a drifting adventure of life. And in the meantime, during that adventure, my husband now, was looking everywhere for me. He had flown to different colleges that I was going to. And he just kept barely missing me. And so, it had been about ten years since we had last seen one another, and he found me on Myspace. And after that, it only took two weeks and I knew it was the right thing and we were married and we'll be married four years on December 16th. Here in a couple weeks. And we have two beautiful little boys, who are two and one. We're really happy. We're not the most romantic couple...we like fishing and camping. And that's our awesome love story.

I love the idea that people can, from time to time, make love out of nothing at all.

During the wild life adjustment which is the first year of college, a friend from high school and I spent a lot of time supporting each other by phone from across state lines. More than once I was the consoling ear as she was dealing with the tormenting jabs of a particularly abrasive fellow student. Some days she was crying and sure that he was destined to destroy her entire college experience, possibly even chasing her out of school altogether.

As we grew more and more comfortable in our new surroundings, we created our own support groups and spoke less. And, unbeknownst to me, the young man reshaped himself. The two became friends. The months turned to years, and the two became more than friends. The years rolled on and they engaged and wed. They've lived happily as a wedded couple— from his first year as a tormentor to present-day loving husband; all without Mr. Darcy's resources.

On the far side of the pursuit spectrum sits Dan. Dan actually espouses the philosophy which Mr. Darcy intoned, "I cannot forget the follies and vices of other so soon as I ought, nor their offenses against myself.

My feelings are not puffed about with every attempt to
move them. My temper would perhaps be called
resentful. My good opinion once lost is lost forever."
He believes that people's orientation toward you can
be easily determined, and is not likely to be changed.
Although this may just be an emotional projection
(he's still peeved at people he knew in the third
grade). The first time Dan invites you out to
something (he's not big on begging), if you say, "Yes,"
that works just fine for him. But, if after accepting the
invite, you flake? It's pretty much game over. He
figures, if you are interested, you will make all
necessary arrangements to come. Lack of arrival
indicates lack of interest. He believes that, if you flake
today, you didn't want to be there... ever. No use
running back.

Dan and I have just moved to D.C. and started
working at a restaurant together. Mostly, the two of
us just worked and kept our heads down. We would
joke around with each other, but most of our co-
workers just didn't understand us. But, there is this
one girl. There's always this one girl, but not usually
for Dan. So Julie and Dan, almost miraculously,
connect. The three of us go out for drinks twice after
work. They talk for a while, and Dan invites her to a
small event we are having. She says she's coming. Our
event comes and she doesn't. I check in with Dan after
the guests leave. He shrugs. "She didn't want to
come." He didn't speak to her again.

Dan doesn't spend a lot of time crushed by unrequited
love.

I, on the other hand, vacationed in that labyrinth from
time to time. I've been on both sides of the maze. But,

during my junior year of college I was definitely the pursuer and kind of an idiot. But, like I said, it's going to be years before I learn anything about quality pursuit.

Starting my undergrad studies, I have a plan in place to meet every single student on that campus. I am an ambitious social force in a small pool of students, and I want to have fun and make sure that everyone else is having fun, too. Not irresponsible, chaotic fun, mostly board games, dinner parties, movie trips, and the occasional, off-campus event.

By year two, I am giving up on my quest to meet every student. I do have a fairly expansive network, and a great group of friends. But, I'm in love with one of them, and she has no idea, because I'm scared by the idea of messing up the group dynamic. I'm also terrified of the idea that she'll reject me. So, I box up my feelings like a pro, and throw myself into being the social coordinator for our little cadre.

When I could be making her feel special, I go out of my way to make her feel like exactly anyone else in the group. I spend a lot of time planning events and outings which I know she likes. But, I never tell her I'm planning them for her. This goes on for over a year. And, now I'm going a little crazy. I finally screw up the courage to tell her that I'm interested, and I plan to tell her tomorrow. Except for one thing; today she confides in me that she has a complicated, "on again, off again" relationship with a guy from her hometown, that right now, she wishes was on. So basically, it's a little late for making her feel special.

I tell her anyway, a few days later. It isn't the
smartest thing I've ever done.
But, I'm still learning. I write this eloquent letter,
enumerating all of my struggles leading to this point
and the depth of my feelings, and I read it to her. She
is shocked, confused, and overwhelmed. After
reflecting, she feels betrayed, because I know her
situation, and am complicating it further. I apologize,
whole-heartedly, and go about the task of making
myself scarce. The remainder of the semester was
fairly uncomfortable as I recused myself as the social
organizer and withdrew into my room and my studies.
Thankfully, there are only a few weeks left in the
school year, and I could get away to stop talking and
do some thinking.

Over the summer I make some interesting life
observations, do some growing, and head back to
college, hoping to win her heart. I resume my duties
as the group facilitator and try out my new, slightly
more grown-up self. Much more deliberately, but,
without seeming too eager, I try to make her feel a
little special, and be there in a way that made me a
little special to her. We have a fairly good senior year.
We go easily from civil back to friends. And we even
approach good friendship by the end. But by then, she
was with the other guy. Me? I was a better person, but
I was definitely on my own.

After graduation, the members of our merry band go
our separate ways. And, while it is hard for me to
contribute my personal touches on her life, I make
sure I keep her at the top of my holiday and birthday
card list. A few years after leaving college, I am
walking the streets of D.C. after work, and I get a call
from her. The substance of the conversation is ten

random minutes of catching up on life, before she asks me about my experiences in The District, explaining that she's applying for a fellowship at a university right here. The two years of silence were over and within those minutes so was the illusion of closure. I spend a few months hoping to hear from her about the position; and a few more just hoping to hear from her. Ultimately, it is years before I see her again, but unbidden, she sneaks into my head from time to time.

As we all know, out of the mouths of children come the best advice. Alec Greven, the nine-year-old whose bestseller *How to Talk to Girls* has sold over 300,000 copies, has some brilliant things to say on the topic of the pursuit of romance. "Getting a girl's attention is a very hard thing and it takes a lot of work [...] Pick a girl in the class. Ask her to be your friend. That's a good start." He goes on to suggest gifts and compliments, but he cautions against trying too hard; warning his readers that this, and other transgressions, could cause a, "straightaway ditch." While, he gives a myriad of ways and reasons to pursue your interest, he is a healthy realist. "Now don't scream if you can't get the girl even after you've tried everything. If it doesn't work out, just let it go."[30]

As a member in good standing of the, "loved and lost club," it's easier to say, than to do.

I still try to win people over, despite the fact that unrequited feelings can be just that. And, maybe Dan is right. I don't know. But Pride and Prejudice would have been a much shorter story if Mr. Darcy had thrown up his hands, "Screw her. I don't have to take this." *The End*

Love Taps

Deep offense at a perceived slight aside, Dan is a fantastic character. He is the epitome of a capable man. He can defend himself, he's handy around the house or workplace, and he's a bit of a romantic, too. When it comes to communication, however, some of his deficiencies creep up. A very particular communicative struggle for Dan was always, the compliment.

It's not that Dan didn't want to tell people nice things. It's just that, when those things came out of his mouth, they never seemed to sound like nice things. When we worked together, I was regularly called upon to deliver the compliments of Dan's heart. "Morris, can you tell the hostess that her new hair is nice, and that it makes her look like a grownup, which will be good, cause maybe people will take her more seriously. But, use nicer words, to not hurt her feelings. "

"Sure, Dan."

From time to time, instead of delivering the compliments for him, I'd help him craft the raw idea into a polished compliment.

"Uh."

"What?"

"That weird pattern on [acquaintance]'s dress, it looks nice on her. How should I say that?"

"Don't say 'weird', and don't say 'on you.' Keep it simple. Try, 'That's a nice dress.' Then shut up."

As Dan's lifelong designated complimenter and compliment consultant, we shared many jokes about the transformation of a compliment from inception to execution. Leaving from his house to pick up his date, he's in the zone, "You look amazing." But as he starts the engine of his car, the focus drifts, "You really look good." When he turns off of his street it's, "That's a nice dress." By the freeway, "You look okay, in that." At the midpoint of the trip we're down to, "At least the dress looks okay." On the exit ramp, "It's a good thing you picked that dress, it distracts from the mess." Pulling into her driveway, "At least you tried." And finally she comes to the door... "Yer face looks like crap."

Dan has improved from those days, however. I doubt that he harbors any dread before complimenting someone; or that any of his recent compliments have made anyone cry. Nevertheless, many relationships have a playfully antagonistic component. Witty jabbing and play fighting are the slow-pitched softballs of makeup sex. Seriously, how many love scenes start with a fight? Dan is an expert at the antagonist part, playful and otherwise. As a result, our apartment was, often enough, a verbal street fight. Dan and his girlfriend, Gillian, were back and forth all the time. Well, maybe it was more like a verbal Sesame Street Fight. A favorite rejoinder tossed around our apartment was, "You're a heaping trashcan of poo!" Erudite, perhaps not, but they soon enough would kiss and make up.

Sometimes, though, you want to reach a little higher with your jabs. At those times, you need a wit sharper than your own. *Downstown*, a comic strip, features a character who rents out his scathing tongue's services for those people without the gift of snark.[31] Then, there's the, *You've Got Mail*, scene with Kathleen Kelly, "What happens to me when I'm provoked is that I get tongue-tied and my mind goes blank." She proceeds to wish for the ability to fire off, Joe Fox-quality zingers. So, occasionally, the best weapon in an argument may be someone else's brain. [32]

Four of us are lounging in the apartment, Dan, his girlfriend, me, and our other roommate. Dan is being Dan, funny by way of vaguely annoying. When his girlfriend made some amusing comment to which Dan took mock offense, he looked over to me, "Morris, insult G's intelligence." I laughed, and returned to whatever I was doing, not wanting to be drawn into their battle. The moment, as so many moments before, was fading out of existence when on the last instant of humorous applicability, our other roommate leans up from his recliner, "You are so stupid..." He begins, startling all of us, "You're so stupid that you are dating my roommate!"

Over-Prepared and Over- Enthusiastic

February 13, 2011

Dear John,

I never really got into Valentine's Day. All the hype and the drama, never turns out to be worth the expectation. Though, our Valentine's Day will definitely be remembered.

I love the fact that you were planning this so far in advance. In the future, however, you should maybe wait 'til the event before you purchase flowers. Roses lose something when their brittle, discolored petals fall off.

The lunch date at [crazy popular restaurant] was a brilliant idea; their sea scallops are miniature bites of sunshine. It was totally weird how they lost your reservation on the most popular dine-out day of the year. The food really smelled amazing while we waited...on standby...for two hours. But seriously, who needs a pricey lunch in a clean environment. That fish fillet sandwich really hit the spot.

When you said we were off to see an afternoon show, I thought you meant matinee in a theater. I think you can understand my surprise when we sat in on a film studies class to watch an art movie. And while I like the art scene as much as the next girl, literally watching film decay doesn't exactly ring my bells. For the next big movie outing, you may want to consider something a little more conventional... like, *No Strings Attached*, I'm just saying.

Our date quickly progressed to lukewarm as dinner wasn't that hot either. I'm mean—who likes a whiner? Seriously. When you send your food back four times on one of the highest volume nights of service even the most patient server or manager is bound to get annoyed. If you don't like what's on the menu, you should either go to a different restaurant or *EAT AT HOME*. Modifying your entrée 800 times is beyond the opposite of sexy. And I know I told you that I enjoy them, but I think the whole thing may have gone better if you hadn't opted for a bagpiper as our serenade option. I honestly don't think our server heard any of the things you said—which is kind of a relief.

We probably should have called it a night at that point, but hindsight is 20/20. Clubbing isn't really my scene, but it seemed to get you into a good place. Liquid courage is a suitable name for it. The first drink was excellent. Then you started lapping me and switched to shots. Better yet, you bought a shot for that girl at the bar when you thought I wasn't looking. Next, you stood on the stool and yelled at the bartender. Then you *bit* the bouncer. You're a grown-ass man and you BIT SOMEONE!!! Which would have been bad enough, had you not asked me for cab fare after you lost your wallet in the process of them throwing you out. I can only assume you made it home safely, since you've been tweeting, texting, emailing, IMing, drunk-dialing, and hung over dialing me since last night.

This would normally be the part where I said we should be friends or something; let's just go with "or something" (a.k.a. Total Strangers). It was very unusual to date you. I wish you all the introspection in the world.

Not Joking Around,

Jane

While it's my earnest hope that you have never received a letter, text, or email like this one, it's usually true that, over a lifetime, a strong majority of us earn at least one black mark in our relational profile. I, myself, have a lot more than one.

Sarah and I hadn't met. We'd facebooked and emailed. But, our schedules didn't sync up well, which is par for the course in my relational existence.

As a people watching, book junky and researcher with a long list of things that I looked for in a partner, I would tend to overdo the pre-date reconnaissance. So, when we finally met up, I casually referenced things like a fundraiser she worked on once in an obscure aspect of her history, Sarah did what any reasonable person might do—politely rebuffed my request for a second date.

In hindsight, I don't really blame her. As a kid fresh out of college, it would be a few years before I'd learn the difference between information and knowledge and even more before I could turn knowledge into wisdom. Though, I did learn a valuable lesson and an easy rule to follow going forward: No matter how little you think you know or how inconsequential the data, don't tell a girl every single thing you know (or figure out) about her on the first date.

If at First You Don't Succeed

It's really quite easy to get intimidated at the prospect of a complicated, labor intensive date. No matter how much time you spend planning, something could go wrong, and then you've got fallout and fallout is the worst. It's easier not to try at all. Dinner and a movie once a month is good enough, because no one likes disappointment. Unfortunately for those of us who hate to be disappointed, most great successes are preceded by pretty spectacular failures.

My great friend and former roommate, Dan, proposed to his wife on their trip to Florida, by scribbling his request on an underwater writing slate after she found the engagement ring in the sand during the second open-water dive of their SCUBA certification.

I think we can all agree that a move of that nature constituted a date full of planning and fraught with risk. But, despite a few small hiccups the result was an unqualified success. Nevertheless, his road to a brilliant underwater marriage proposal experienced its share of bumps in the paving process.

Dan is famous for his hard exterior. A backroom poker player, a small-time MMA fighter, and general scrapper who, at six feet tall, his closely cropped haircut and army surplus camo pants cuts a rather intimidating figure. Dan isn't the person others presume is a lover. He's better known for things like K.O.-ing a guy in an altercation over a parking space. But, judgment lapses aside, a few of us know that deep, deep down, Dan has quite the softer side.

Dan had been dating this girl from college and he was looking to create a truly epic date. He plotted and planned for weeks. His somewhat estranged father was living in a gated community off of a lake. Even though the beach of the lake was poorly maintained, it had a bare gazebo and potential, and that was all Dan needed.

On the condition that he not use the house, Dan's dad gave him access to the lake and the grounds. Dan raked sand for days to clear crabgrass and debris and turn a dicey patch of earth into a magazine worthy beach. He wrapped reflective and sheer material around the entire gazebo, leaving a perfect opening facing the lake and the setting sun. He had artificial vines and flowers on all of the beams, and tea candles perched on every beam and rafter positioned to reflect into the dining area when the sun finally went down. By the time he finished work on that area, it looked like outdoor seating for a restaurant at a resort. The prep work was done, all that remained was execution.

Normally I'd be his point man on an event of this magnitude, but I was 300 miles away at college. So, he went with what he had. He actually paid my youngest brother Nick to wait on them to preserve the dining out experience. But, he was going to need food to serve. Dan had planned as much of that as he could. He picked out a restaurant with a great curbside take-out service, and commissioned his two siblings to drive to the restaurant, pick up the food, and bring it to his beautiful beach date spot.

Dan's brother and sister made it to the restaurant, but at that point, the assignment started to get the better of them. Instead of taking advantage of the quick take-out option, they put their names on the list at the hostess's stand, and after forty minutes of waiting, the realization strikes them that continuing along their current trajectory would almost certainly make them late for the rendezvous. They called an audible.

"What's the new play," you ask?
1. Go to the store; pick up two raw steaks, and a few random sides.
2. ...
3. Hand off the prepared foods, to be served.

So, the pair dash into the nearest grocery store to execute their new plan. And, after exhausting the entire budget and all the just in case money for this project, they head out to pick up Nick, Dan's server for the evening.

In the meantime, Dan had setup all of the sand-filled paper bags, so that when his accomplices got back from their other assignments, they could simply light the tea candles and drop them in to create the pristine lit walkway, to the pavilion full of tea candles. He hopped in his car to drive the 30 minutes to the home of his early to bed girlfriend, who was already none too thrilled that she would be out after the sun went down (between you and me, I think she was scared of vampires). Retrieving her from beneath the withering glares of her disapproving family members, Dan turned around to head back to the lake, the gazebo, and to vindication, in the form of this super date.

As he pulled up to the site, Dan was deeply concerned at the still unlit lanterns lining the walkway and, leading his date to the gazebo he grew more and more doubtful of the evening ending well, as he stared at the desolately hollow shell of the shelter which was meant to be warmly inviting and to bring a deeply romantic ambience to bear. Entering the little nook, all of Dan's fears are confirmed. No Candles. No Server. No Food. Knowing that this wasn't going to break his way, he gave Annie an imagination only tour of the date that might have been. Then the two drove to the last place Dan wanted to be at that moment, his dad's off limits house.

He pushed open the door to witness Hurricane Siblings in progress. Two steaks sitting raw on a grill without propane, shrimp sautéed in pan growing cold on the stove, a plate of premade pinwheel rolls, and every pot and pan in the house were strewn about the kitchen. Dan stopped himself just short of reading the Riot Act, but threw a few verbal jabs at the complete failing on their part.

Dan calls for a mulligan, and after collecting the edible remains of the dinner, left his sister and brother in the chaos, took my brother and headed back to the site just in time to miss the sunset and sit for a few uncomfortable minutes before diving into the pseudo-dinner. After foregoing food for the entire day in anticipation of their date, shrimp and a pinwheel appetizer failed to slake Annie's hunger. Eventually the date was put out of its misery as Dan shuffled the other two into his car and drove the two and a half hours to drop off the still hungry Annie and then Nick. Far from over, Dan continues what has devolved into a day-long driving expedition, and returns to the scene of the crime.

His return marks the next disheartening discovery of this unimaginably long day. After being discovered in the midst of their failure, the fear of Dan's wrath overcame his siblings who, squandering their chances of atonement, fled leaving Dan as the sole casualty of their hurricane forces.

As the laborious process of bringing order to chaos began, Dan's father entered the house he had been promised would be untouched and stared silently into the kitchen he reasonably assumed would be just as clean as when he left. No real surprise registered on his face at the sight of his disturbed and occupied kitchen. The only reaction, in fact the only communication was the ever so slight narrowing of his eyes and the rippling twitch of the muscle at his jaw line.

By the time the wreckage had been utterly cleared, and no trace of the fiasco remained, Dan was headed not to bed, but to work, where he would endure a long day of semi-conscious actions and reactions and persistent reflection on the previous night.

It seems as though the adage, "The best laid plans of mice and men, often go awry," had a child with, "Murphy's Law," and that child was Dan's super date. And, he still went on to do great, complicated, and adventurously romantic things.

The Drunk Prude

A restaurant is a world unto itself. It has its own rhythm of living. Its morning is a banker's afternoon, and the banker's bedtime is the servers' power hour. And days off at the bank are the busiest restaurant days. As a result, restaurant people spend an awful lot of time with others of their kind, both inside and outside work. In all my years and in every restaurant, that was true, restaurant people exist together.

Of course, I think there is an element of surviving restaurants that make it safer to hang together. Unrelenting exposure to the full and bizarre spectrum of humanity, including people whose partners say things like, "My wife doesn't talk to the help," and others who leave you nothing after almost $500 of the best service possible, crushes your soul like that guy in *The Crucible*.[33] On the other hand a guest can give you thirty bucks on his ten dollar check just because the two of you clicked. It's a lot like drawing a card in a board game; you're never quite sure what you're in for. That unpredictability, among other elements of the job, affects people in deep ways.

A lot of people have written humorous accounts of food service shenanigans, and while none of the places I've worked were of the sort to take revenge on you through your food (spitting, etc.), there was a consistent element of hard living. From caffeine to coke, we ran the gamut on self-medication. While the closest I came to illegal was having a friend blow pot smoke in my face, my drinking and my serving had an easily arguable causal relationship.

A funny thing about me is that deep down I'm judgmental, intolerant of willful ignorance, and a little bit prudish. It's only funny because I can usually keep a lid on it and let it out in witty doses. Occasionally, it bubbles over and I get too caustic, but a few days of total isolation usually helps. Another thing that can bring out those qualities in me is booze.

After working six consecutive shifts in a row together, a handful of us want to spend the first of two days off, hung-over. Well, we don't actually say that. What we say is, "Jules said, pick up a bottle of wine and come hang out after work, she's got the new place, so no one needs to risk a DUI." Distracted by excitement at the upcoming days off, I do exactly that, buy a bottle of wine and head over to her place.

When I arrive, it is clear that I have distinctly misinterpreted the primary aim of this gathering. DVR-ed recordings of a comic talk show drone in succession like some kind of a poorly coordinated impromptu marathon, while some of the gathered start making out on chairs and couches, their already half-emptied wine bottles standing like absurd sentries, unobtrusive, but available at a moment's notice. A very small knot of guests occupies the patch of carpet near the television. After a perfunctory greeting, I head for the knot, and for the lack of an alternative, I join their conversation and start in on my bottle of wine.

Several hours into the night (the host of the talk show, I believe, is on her fifth or sixth outfit) the enthusiasm for the pseudo-silent event wanes and many of the group begin to leave. I accept the offer to crash for the night and am offered a side room in which to sleep. My progress down the hall is irregular as I combat the effect of the wine I've consumed. I'm standing at the couch emptying my pockets and preparing to lie down, when in comes another server. Instead of the unoccupied couch, she crosses the tiny room and grabs me around the neck, as though to regain some stability against her chemically altered gait. Her next words shatter my illusion, "We should hook up." She slurs matter-of-factly.

My inner prude is screaming a thousand arguments into my ear in rapid succession, but after the better part of a bottle of wine, I seem to have lost my command of language. "No, we shouldn't," I finally manage; pleased with my tiny success.

"Why not, am I not pretty?"

My bias toward truthfulness almost results in my telling her that she is in fact quite pretty, but this time the slowness of my tongue works to my distinct advantage. Concentrating hard, I return to my original point, side-stepping the question altogether. "You have a boyfriend," I reply. My great overestimation of her state is reflected in my follow up, "How would this make him feel?"

"Jarred would be fine with it," comes her instant slurred response. I'm not sure if her sudden jerking movement was by alcohol, design, or both, but my focus on speaking has left me unprepared, and I fall backwards onto the waiting couch. The too-low couch does nothing to aid my attempts at fleeing, and I continue to reason with her as the room fades in and out of focus.

I'm struggling to stand, and to make my words understood when I see movement through the open door. One of the guys who works at the restaurant's bar is walking down the hall, hand in hand with a woman server. After ushering her into the bedroom, he turns back to face me, all smiles. Despite the look of horror I can feel on my face, he leans into the room and flicks the light switch. I can just make out his smile as he whispers, "Aww yeah, Mo," and closes the door with a tiny click.

In the darkness, I abandon all pretense, squirming as quickly as my impaired brain and body will allow, I make it to the end of the couch and lurch into a standing position. When I turn the lights back on, she recoils from the brightness. "First," I start out, the adrenaline of the moment having cleared out my brain. "You have a boyfriend. And, making out with a stand-in when he's not around is childish and selfish. Second, you and I are not dating. And, even if you do this at other times, with other people, I'm not other people. I don't "hook-up" with people, especially if we're not in a relationship." I'm on a roll now, "Jarred is my friend anyway, this is ridiculous. And, seriously! If he ever decided to take this out on me, he's like six inches taller than me and is mostly muscle."

Stopping the stream of meanness I fear will come next, I offer her my hand. "I think you really just need to go to sleep."

She begins to protest as I lay her down on the other couch, but before she can complete a thought, she begins the regular breathing of sleep.

"Is this what people do?" My mind is racing after this experience. I think of the bartender and the server in the next room, "Are my peers so lonely that anyone is better than no one at all?"

I hold her hand for a few more minutes to make sure she's done for the evening, and turn the room's light off for a final time, return to my couch, and lie down.

"I don't mind being alone," I think. "I'll wait."

Almost a Schoolyard Romance

In the fifth grade, my parents sent me and my siblings to a small private school near our house. As an unusual young man just entering the awkward pubescent years, starting a new school was exciting, and a guaranteed challenge.

Now, when I assert that I was an unusual kid, I'm not playing up the hype. I'm understating the strangeness. My two favorite activities at --that age were playing chess and reading. My heroes, Arthur Conan Doyle's Sherlock Holmes and Star Trek's Mr. Spock, encouraged me to a life of observation and reflection. A thinking, chess playing, eyebrow-raising child who threw around phrases like, "It's elementary," and "Affirmative" had a lot of time to philosophize, on his own.

My observations on love, and the comings and goings of life led me to the conclusion that romances which predate the latter half of high school were, realistically, doomed. Picture an eleven-year-old kid trying to convince a group of his "changing" classmates that dating is counterproductive to the process of self-discovery. I got a lot of questions, curious glances, and even nods acknowledging the sound nature of my logic, but not nearly as many converts to my way of thinking. The problem with being an overly logical child in puberty is that if you don't want to date, you spend a lot of time crushing quietly.

In the fifth and sixth grade, I had a crush on this girl, we'll call her Sue. Sue was a really nice girl; kind of opinionated and cute. She challenged me to a rope jumping competition in fifth grade. I won handily, thanks to my father's old school sports training. After that, we chatted with some regularity, to the chagrin of her boyfriend. Being in the fifth grade, it was only a matter of time before candy became a topic of conversation. At one point, she explained to me that she hated grape flavored candy. Being a logical child, I said something eloquent, "Yeah, grape candy sucks!"

There's one problem with my saying, "Yeah, grape candy sucks!" I believed that, you should do what you say. And, I'd just said, I didn't like grape candy. I immediately developed a deep hatred for grape candy, and was an adult before I had another piece. It was a Blow Pop, and it was great.

I was home on a visit after college, and I ran into Sue at a movie theatre. A lot of stuff fades in a decade, but the first thing that popped into my head when I saw her, was the "Grape Candy Exaggeration." I doubt Sue even remembered that I didn't like grape candy. Either way, she wouldn't have been able to convince me to give up grape candy again. And even though I don't much care for grape candy (Blow Pops, being a notable exception), I'm not crushing on Sue anymore either.

I had, mostly, gotten over my crush on Sue by the eighth grade. I had found my next true "like," we'll call her, Ann. Ann and I didn't have the rope jumping connection, but when your entire graduating class is less than 40 students, you get to know about everyone. Ann was nice to me, even when other members of my class were less so. In hindsight, perhaps she was just defending a slightly bullied new-ish kid. But I fell for her, like only a middle school boy can.

Being in the final stretch of middle school, it was extremely difficult to toe the hard line of not dating, and I even lost track of it for a few moments that year. As an ex-homeschooler in junior high, smooth I was not. Smart? Yeah! Nice? Absolutely! Occasionally, I was even funny. But smoothness was a trait well beyond my grasp. So, when I decided to try and make my affections to Ann known, I didn't know what to do. There wasn't much chance of my just telling her what I was thinking and feeling. I hadn't progressed much beyond my Batman years in terms of that particular brand of conversation.

With conversation off the table, I thought flowers would serve my end. Now, I know what you're thinking, "Women like flowers. Great plan kid." Yeah, but when I pirated a single carnation from the funeral I attended two days ago, it didn't exactly send the message I had in my mind. Less so when instead of handing it to her, I wedged it through the handle of her locker, before school started...and then never mentioned it.

I did, finally get around to saying something to Ann. And, by "saying something" I mean, "gave her a note." And, by "gave" I mean, "handed it to someone. Who handed it to someone. Who handed it to her, while we were on our tour bus for the class trip in D.C." I, obviously, didn't just jump right in, and tell her that I liked her. We passed a few notes worth of inane chit chat, and then I asked her if, maybe, we could do

something together, some time, 'cause I kinda liked
her.

When I got back an enthusiastic "yes," response, I was
too distracted to notice that the handwriting was
completely different. And that the person who signed
it, wasn't her... it was a boy whose name began with
the same letter as hers, next to whom, she just
happened to be sitting.

I was a little hurt. By the time we got back from our
trip, I'd, once again, given up the idea of dating before
the end of high school. And I guess, in the long run,
that is okay. I wouldn't recommend it for everyone.
But, it made me the person I am. The person who
finally figured out that, talking is more important
than a flower in a locker, and that it pays to have
fewer people between you and the person to whom
you're talking. I learned a lot more stuff between fifth
grade and now; but those are stories for other
chapters, books, or the quiet of my own mind.

Deal Breakers

What is it about "deal breakers?" Things so important in our romantic identity that, in no small way, our love lives are defined by the very particular things we don't want in them. Definition by void. You have yours. She has hers. He has his. And, God knows, I have mine. I'm a left-leaning independent, so she can't be too conservative. But I think the system is fatally flawed, so she can't get too caught up in the political noise. As a listed deal breaker, a female friend of mine had to include, grind dancing with other girls, in her list of deal breakers...because one of her dates did it in front of her. People's tics and habits are deal breakers as well. A friend of mine and I decided that we could never "live happily ever after," because I violently shake my leg when I'm seated. And then of course, there's THE habit.

In the video store, I saw this woman. She was quite attractive and seemed to be, at least relatively, charming. The two of us engaged in an ever so small round of flirtation. She smiled. I smiled back. It was a fun sort of eye catch tag held throughout the store. I wanted to ask for her number, but wasn't ready. I mean, I didn't have a plan, an out, or even an idea of where to go if she said yes. So I didn't say anything, but I didn't give up either. I got to the counter to check out first but took my precious time actually departing. I needed to go to the store just a few doors down and so I sauntered and meandered to see what would happen. I was ambling up the sidewalk away from the video store when I saw her come out and I stopped. If she didn't bolt for her car, I was going to ask for her number and invite her for coffee across the street. I was looking for fiddling keys. I turned toward her as I saw her sit down on one of the benches in front of the store. I was already walking back that way when she lit her cigarette. I did a mid-stride 180 and headed to the destination store.

At this point, it didn't matter if she was the Cristo-centric, intellectually curious, left-leaning, musician, entrepreneurial business owning daughter of a billionaire investing genius; she puffs. And this is one of those things at which the line is drawn. Smoking... I just can't handle it. What is it about "deal breakers?" I wish there was some way around it for me, but it has been and will be a deal breaker. Something about kissing a smoker leaves a bad taste in my mouth.

So, is that what love is? Trying so hard to avoid some things so that what is left over is good enough? I have a friend whose list of deal breakers includes, "having or wanting children", "any unfaithfulness", AAAAND "being an Ohio State fan." The whole thing is a little daunting. You can be disqualified from a relationship for things so far beyond the realm of your control that they don't even show up on your own internal radar.

Saying, "No" to things can be a really healthy thing. People make dangerous and unhealthy compromises, and it's definitely important not to put yourself in positions which would leave you miserable in your relationship. At the same time, make sure that your only definition isn't definition by void; be sure that you are running toward something attainable.

It's in the Tones

I want to talk about music for a bit. Music is the first part of the world I understood. On my mother's side of the family, music was the lubricant which let all the different pieces move. One of the early memories of my youth was standing in front of the extended family to demonstrate my newly developed skills of harmonization. It was a sort of confirmation for us. We sang; we listened, we watched. And, very early in my life, music became the new pulse of my beating heart.

Many people are fixated on specific genres of music. From what I can tell, this is the result of perceived or desired identification with the artist or artist type, or a desire to avoid identification with another. This is an entirely understandable way by which individuals develop their own personal music appreciation, as it, by extension, satisfies the psychological desire to be understood. One's belief that the artist has formed the words that tell one's story can create both an attachment to the artist, and more, the belief that people will now understand this person's experience through this music.

My eclectic tastes have likely evolved from the same basic principles. While I find strong identification in many individual lyrics and melody lines, I fail to feel the complete connection to any one artist or even one genre. As such, I began to fall in love with the individual elements of music that bring genres together. I started to love the lyrics that transcend different personal experiences and thus different genres. Music came alive to me.

Isn't it amazing how overwhelming it can be to listen to a big band rendition of a classic jazz piece? The sound hits you like a wave, threatening to wash you away forever. But then, as the wave recedes, the experience moves to the next level. Now, the undertow of the song comes full circle and tickles your back as you hear the "oh so subtle" tones of the violins, holding you up and giving you nothing but air to walk on. Until the piano brings you back, as if you're descending on a flight of stairs, walking you down a spiral of dreams and soft touches, while the warm sound of bass are caressing in deep, deep tones. It's overwhelming and it swallows you whole.

Of course, lyrics take the tension of the notes, and transfers it into our mouths. Lyrics of love, hate, loneliness, desire, rejection, triumph, and failure the list would go on forever.

"I'll need you, feed you, even let you hold the remote control."
-Adam Sandler (Grow Old With You)
"Since you've been gone I can breathe for the first time."
-Kelly Clarkson
"Ain't no sunshine when she's gone, only clouds when she's away."
-Bill Withers
"As I fail miserably, tryin' to get the girl all the bad guys want."
-Bowling for Soup
"Afraid and shy, I let my chance go by; the chance that you might love me too."

-Michael Buble (You Don't Know Me)
"Oh, what a beautiful sight, and I'm not such a clumsy guy, if I really try. I can really fly a [kite]."
-Clark Gesner (The Kite)
"Yeah and all of these bastards, have taken his place. He's forgotten but not yet gone."
-Ben Folds (Fred Jones Pt. 2)
"No, they can't take that away from me."
Ira Gershwin
Lyrics have the capacity to capture the human experience in a way that leaves the hollow platitudes behind, to touch nerves. It's a beautiful pain. Ben Folds opens one of his songs with this amazing line, "I feel like a quote out of context." How many people lacked the words to express that, until they heard that song? Music offered the subconscious a chance to be known.

"Let music live!"

The Last First Kiss

First kisses are fascinating. There can be a lot of
mental build up leading to that kiss. Some first kisses
are the overture in what will be the show of a lifetime.
Other kisses are the entire first scene in a short film.
Either way, there's a lot of weight on the first kiss.

My most memorable first kiss was one of those scenes
from a short. Kate and I had been out a couple of
times, and we were having more than our fair share of
fun tooling around D.C. I didn't plan to kiss her that
night. But, I didn't plan not to, either.

I picked her up at her end of the yellow line, and we
came back to Metro Center. We saw a movie at the
Gallery Place Theater. We walked over to Vapiano. I'd
never been before and I kept referring to it as *Via
Piano*. She thought I was being cute and laughed. So I
kept it up through the evening. And, it was a lovely
dinner. After dinner, we metro-ed out to the
Smithsonian.

Most people visit the monuments in the mornings and
the afternoons. They get all the history and miss the
beauty. I took Kate there at ten at night, on a late
summer's evening. We walked through the
magnificent shadow of the Washington Monument, to
the open air corridor of the beautiful WWII Memorial.
As we strolled through tiny pools of artificial light, we
admired the workmanship. Swapping road trip stories
as we looked at each of the state wreaths, we made

our way around the outside. We finally ended up
sitting on the ledge of the fountain, at the heart of the
memorial.

Perched on the lip of the pool, we just took it all in.
The glory of the starry night above us, the majesty of
The Washington Monument in front of us, The
Reflecting Pool and The Lincoln Monument behind us,
the gravity of the World War II Memorial surrounding
us, the beauty of the under-lit jets of water from the
fountain at our feet, and the juxtaposed humor of the
slightly awkward ducks waddling into and out of it
made this the moment. And, I kissed her. It was
beautiful. Like something straight out of a movie. We
walked back to the station to be on the last trains to
our respective destinations.

It was a great scene. It just turned out to be a part of a
much shorter show than I'd imagined.

The first kiss my wife and I shared was not that
impressive. It was not a letdown. But, it wasn't
magical, either. We were a few months (yes, months)
into our great relationship before it actually
happened. We had both been in relationships where
the physical aspect of the budding relationship
overshadowed the emotional, intellectual, and
spiritual aspects. Believing that what we had was
really special, neither of us wanted to risk that
happening here.

In an effort to forestall the deterioration into a
relationship built on the physical, we constructed all
these rules regarding our physical relationship. So
there we were months into the relationship, not
having kissed. And, it sucked. I would kiss her on the

cheek, or forehead. But, we didn't share a true kiss. The rules created an artificial distance that added stress and turned us into legalistic crazy people.

One evening, after watching a DVD, Jess and I were tangled up on the couch. I looked at her. She looked beautiful. We were both happy. I wanted to kiss her; and I didn't. Then I got annoyed. Annoyed, because the rules we set up weren't helping us understand each other. The rules hadn't really kept the physical from crowding out the other parts; it was just diluting things in other ways. They started out as somewhat useful guidelines, but had grossly outlived their utility.

So out of the overflow of my exasperation, I kissed her. The earth didn't move. My heart didn't stop. The sky didn't come tum-b-ling down - tum-b-ling down. On the other hand, the earth didn't swallow us up. We didn't break up. I didn't feel guilty. I just felt relieved. I felt like we could go back to developing our relationship organically, like we probably should have been all along. Because, if it takes a rule or law to make you do what's right for you. Maybe it's not actually right for you.

So, my first kiss with Jess was unremarkable. It was barely a chord in the overture. But, the work as a whole is shaping up to be a legen...wait for it...dary tale of love and woe and lives and sacrifice and challenge and triumph, among other things. If the trade is a so-so first kiss in exchange for the relationship of a lifetime; I'll make that trade all day. Considering the overall trajectory of our relationship, I'm pretty sure Jess would agree.

About the Author

Morris DuBose v.3.0 is a relational expert that provides a youthful yet thought-provoking spin on the ins and outs of people and their relationships with one another. From friendships to dating to the dramatic dive into the marriage realm, DuBose has experienced it all. Still muddling his way along the path of a confused 20 something, with all conundrums and contradictions, he's not black and white, but he hopes to be read all over. When his keyboard is on vacation (or on strike), he spends his time learning his way around central Indiana with his wife Jess.

Pick his brain on MoTheThird.blogspot.com.

OK. So, I have an irrational fear of being sued, and the laws surrounding fair use, while easy to understand, in theory, is not as simple in practice. I figured an extensive notes section would be a good first step.

Notes

[1] *Shrek*. Dir. Andrew Adamson and Vicky Jenson. Perf. Mike Myers, Eddie Murphy, Cameron Diaz. DreamWorks, 2001. Film.
If you haven't seen *Shrek* yet, stop reading and watch this movie… On second thought, keep reading, and just make a mental note to see it.

[2] Cook, Dane, perf. *Retaliation*. Rec. 2004. 2005. CD.
While I have mixed feelings about his total body of work, Dane Cook's track "L-O-V-E" on the "Need" disk of his *Retaliation* album is one of my all time favorites.

[3] *Hitch*. Dir. Andy Tennant. Perf. Will Smith, Eva Mendes, Kevin James. Overbrook Entertainment, 2005. DVD.
I've started making little hash marks on the inside of my DVD case every time I watch this movie. I'm up to 16 marks.

[4] *Mr. & Mrs. Smith*. Dir. Doug Liman. By Simon Kinberg. Perf. Angelina Jolie, Brad Pitt. 20th Century Fox, 2005. DVD.
The film that built a "Brangelina"

[5] *Home Alone*. Dir. Chris Columbus. By John Hughes. Perf. Macaulay Culkin. 20th Century Fox, 1990. Videocassette.
In his defense, Kevin wasn't exploring sex, he was just nosing around his brother's abandoned room being grossed out by naked women.

[6] *Saved!* Dir. Brian Dannelly. By Brian
Dannelly and Michael Urban. Perf. Jena Malone,
Mandy Moore, Macaulay Culkin, Eva Amurri.
United Artists, 2004. Film.
I wish this movie was more hyperbolic.

[7] Dobson, James. *Preparing for Adolescence.*
Ventura, California: Regal, 1989. Print.

[8] *Dictionary.com Unabridged.* Random House,
Inc. 18 Mar. 2014.

[9] *You've Got Mail.* By Nora Ephron. Dir. Nora
Ephron. Perf. Tom Hanks, Meg Ryan. Warner
Bros., 1998. DVD.
The anachronic sounds of dial-up, superimposed
over the also anachronic world of bookstores
before e-readers, superimposed over a
hilarious love story. Go watch it.

[10] Lewis, Michelle Lia., and Andrew
Bryant. *Flirting 101: How to Charm Your Way to
Love, Friendship, and Success.* New York: St.
Martin's Griffin, 2005. Print.

[11] Three 6 Mafia. *It's Hard out Here for a
Pimp.* DJ Paul, Jucy Jay, 2005. CD.
With respect to DJ Paul, Juicy J, and Cedric
Coleman, I really feel like there are a lot of
people for whom it's harder out there.

[12] C.K., Louis. "Oh My God." *Oh My God.* HBO.
2013. Web.

[13] Carnegie, Dale. *How to Win Friends and
Influence People.* New York: Simon and
Schuster, 1981. *Ramon Thomas.* Web. 21 Mar.
2014.

OK let me start by saying, despite its sleazy sounding title, this may be the greatest primer on interpersonal relations ever written despite the fact that it's almost 80 years old. I've read it twice from cover to cover. I leant out my physical copy, or I would have cited the book. Don't hold it against me.

[14] Lewis, Michelle Lia., and Andrew Bryant. See #10

[15] Greene, Fran. *The Flirting Bible: Your Ultimate Photo Guide to Reading Body Language, Getting Noticed, and Meeting More People than You Ever Thought Possible.* Beverly, MA: Fair Winds, 2010. Print.

[16] We've covered this one already. It's the same book from the mystery dinner, and the earlier citation. #10 and #14

[17] Pease, Allan, and Barbara Pease. *Why Men Don't Have a Clue and Women Always Need More Shoes: The Ultimate Guide to the opposite Sex.* New York: Broadway, 2004. Print.

[18] Cox, Tracey. *Superflirt.* London: Dorling Kindersley, 2003. Print.

[19] Greven, Alec. *How to Talk to Girls.* New York: Collins, 2008. Print.
At nine years old, Alec has more to teach up about becoming a man worth dating, than many of the professionals.
[20] Lorre, Chuck, and Bill Prady. *The Big Bang Theory.* CBS. N.d. Television.
"Bazinga!"

---

[21] *Hitch* (2005)
What beats Kevin James doing, "The Q-tip"

[22] Pease, Barbara, and Allan Pease. *Why Men Don't Listen & Women Can't Read Maps: How We're Different and What to Do about It*. New York, NY: Welcome Rain, 2000. Print.
The early book by this relational power couple. It's a little more academic, but still worth the read.

[23] Deborah Tannen, PhD is a Professor of Linguistics at Georgetown University. Her work on relational communication is incredible.
Tannen, Deborah. *You Just Don't Understand: Women and Men in Conversation*. New York, NY: Morrow, 1990. Print.
[24] *Proverbs*. *New American Standard Bible*. N.p.: n.p., n.d. *Bible Gateway*. Web. 22 Mar. 2014.

[25] Bays, Carter, and Craig Thomas. *How I Met Your Mother*. CBS. N.d. Television.
For all the chaos of their episodes, this is a show that knows how to bring a tangent full circle.

[26] *Wedding Crashers*. Dir. David Dobkin. By Steve Faber and Bob Fisher. Perf. Vince Vaughn, Owen Wilson. New Line Cinema, 2005. DVD.

[27] *Spanglish*. By James L. Brooks. Dir. James L. Brooks. Perf. Adam Sandler,. Columbia Tristar, 2004. DVD.
This is, far and away, my favorite Adam Sandler movie. It manages to be over the top and subtle at the same time. I recommend it.

---

[28] Batman, created by Bob Kane is one of the
first and most enduring characters in the
history of comic books. He's always on guard.
And, even when he's playing the part of a
philanderer and party host, he's really just
suppressing the urge to rain down fist-powered
justice on the enemies of his city.

[29] Austen, Jane. *Pride and Prejudice.* New York:
Scholastic Inc, 2007. Print
My first exposure with Pride and Prejudice was
walking in as my sister put in the second of
the two VHS set. Thus, I was robbed of the
initial loathing one is supposed to feel
against Mr. Darcy. I love the story
nonetheless.
[30] See 19
[31] Downs, Tim. *The Laylo Papers*. N.p.:
Communications Center, 1989. Print.
[32] See 9. And by, "See 9," I mean, go watch the
movie.
[33] Miller, Arthur. *The Crucible: A Play in Four
Acts*. New York: Viking, 1953. Print.